Circle of Fire

THE SYMBOLISM & PRACTICES OF WICCAN RITUAL

Sorita D'Este & David Rankine

Published by Avalonia

BM Avalonia
London
WC1N 3XX
England, UK

www.avaloniabooks.co.uk

First Edition May 2005
Copyright © David Rankine and Sorita D'Este

Design by Avalonia
All illustrations, including cover design by Satori, with the exception of
p.123 & 124 by Brian Andrews.

ISBN 1-905297-04-01

Circle of Fire

THE SYMBOLISM & PRACTICES OF WICCAN RITUAL

Sorita D'Este & David Rankine

Guide O fire the seeker
On a path of illumination
On a path through the mysteries
Through the circles of time and space
Through the passions of a loving embrace
Truthful path of perfect will
Mysteries from the cauldron spill

DEDICATION

This book is dedicated to the beautiful members of VITRIOL Grove and the hidden children of the Stone of the Stars. Blessed Be.

"Open your eyes and you will see that the door has been opened and the world of the Gods lies within: and your spirit, rejoicing in this vision, will find itself drawn onwards and upwards."

Greco-Egyptian Magical Papyri
(Unknown Translation)

Table of Contents

Introduction

Wicca is a religion for today and tomorrow. Its simple effectiveness and organic beauty combine to make its appeal grow greater as we move further into the twenty-first century, with its bombardment of technology and overwhelming tide of images.

One of the strengths of Wicca is that it draws from the great magickal traditions of the past, using what has been repeatedly demonstrated to work, to provide a very efficient and elegant way of performing ritual. The need for more ritual in modern life to restore a sense of sacredness to life, communion with the immanent and transcendent divine, and the fellowship of community with peers cannot be overstated.

Wicca is a mystery tradition which facilitates growth of the spirit, something the modern world needs very badly. It helps bring the sense of mystery back into life which we often lose when we move from childhood into adulthood in our materialistic society.

Wicca is constantly growing and evolving; fulfilling people's need for magick, mysticism and religion in their lives, and putting the responsibility for spiritual growth and fulfillment back with the individual. It also encourages the individual to investigate their own role in the web of life, and to develop their connection with and understanding of nature. In Wicca the emphasis is on you to follow your path and grow into the possibilities you can create.

In this book we explore the techniques used in Wiccan ceremonies today, together with the symbolism and purpose of each ritual component. So often rituals are adapted with little or no regard for the purpose and symbolism which play such an important part in magickal ritual, and we hope that the material presented within this volume will help the reader gain insights that will lead to a greater understanding and creative and effective application of the rituals of Wicca.

The history of the tradition is not within the scope of this book, although it is of course both interesting and important to know more about the history of a tradition you follow. What is vital about Wicca is that it works effectively as a beautiful and effective spiritual system for those practicing it. Most of the techniques used within Wiccan ritual have their roots in much older practices, some dating back as far as 5000 years ago. We explore this in our book "*Wicca – Magickal Beginnings*".

May the Goddess and God bless you and guide you on your path though the mysteries.

Sorita D'Este & David Rankine
May 2005

PART I - The Foundations

What is Wicca?

Wicca encompasses your whole worldview and way of life, and is always there in the way you look at and interact with the world.

Wicca is an experiential spiritual system of magick and ceremony that works with the divine as both Goddess and God, and emphasises growth through balance and discipline. This balance, be it of light and dark, feminine and masculine, or active and passive, acts as a dynamic tension to create harmony and enable the individual to progress in their development through understanding their relationship with themselves and the world around them.

The celebration of the Goddess and God is at the heart of Wicca. The patron Goddess of Wicca is usually associated with the Moon, although she is also often seen as having stellar, terrestrial and chthonian forms. The patron God of Wicca is usually associated with forests, plants and animals; he is also sometimes seen as having solar and chthonian forms.

The core ethical philosophy of Wicca is contained within the Wiccan Rede: - "*An It Harm None, Do As Ye Will*". This is an ethical guide for the individual, which stresses the need for the individual to take personal responsibility for their actions, and the consequences thereof. The morality of Wicca is life-positive, with an emphasis on fulfilling personal potential and radiating a positive influence into the world.

The Wheel of the Year Sabbats

Wiccans celebrate the eight seasonal festivals which are better known as the *Wheel of the Year*. These festivals mark the changing seasons and bring practitioners to a closer understanding of nature.

The Wheel of the Year Sabbats are:
Samhain (Halloween) October 31
Yule (Winter Solstice) December 21
Imbolc (Candlemas) Feb 1
Ostara (Spring Equinox) March 21

Beltane (May Day) May 1
Litha (Summer Solstice) June 21
Lughnasadh (Lammas) August 1
Modron (Autumn Equinox) September 21

Please note that the dates given are for the Northern Hemisphere, as the seasons in the Southern Hemisphere are reversed, so too are the festivals. Also keep in mind that the dates for the Solstices and Equinoxes may vary from year to year, so it is important to consult an astrological calendar for the exact dates each year.

Esbats

Some covens and solitaries also hold rituals at the Full Moon and other lunar phases, in addition to the Wheel of the Year celebrations. These ceremonies, which are commonly known as "esbats" are often centred on results magick such as healing, as well as devotional workings.

Rites of Passage

Initiation rites are usually practiced by those working within covens, during which the initiate is welcomed into the group and tradition in a formal ceremony. The new initiate also makes their own personal commitment towards both the tradition and the group known during such a ceremony, in addition to their commitment to the Goddess and God. Further initiations are undertaken to mark specific points during the cycle of learning and experience, which may lead to a person eventually moving on and starting a coven of their own.

Solitary practitioners of the Wiccan tradition may make similar commitments in self-dedication ceremonies. During such a ceremony the practitioner makes a personal commitment to the Goddess and God and to themselves towards fulfilling their own personal goals of following the Wiccan path.

Although this serves a similar function to that of initiation into a coven it is important to stress that the two are not the same. Self-dedication is a solitary pursuit, which is between the practitioner and their Gods, whereas initiation into a coven is done in the presence of the Gods and peers.

There are benefits to both paths, as well as pitfalls; most members of covens also work solitary, some solitaries may find a coven after years of solitary practice and become a coven initiate. In addition, some coven initiates decide for one reason or another that solitary work is better suited to them and go solo. Some people switch between the two paths or work them concurrently for a lifetime. You need to decide which is best suited to your lifestyle, development and needs.

The method of learning and experiencing ritual is also very different. The solitary practitioner will need to learn his or her rituals from books, workshops and possibly through attending public ceremonies. The coven initiate will learn through example - that is they will see the way in which ritual is performed within their coven and will learn through experience. This may be complemented by additional solitary study.

Most Wiccan covens work with a three degree system of initiation, with some having a fourth stage at the start which is usually called "Dedication" – being a dedication to the coven and to learning after which the new member becomes a probationer to the coven, undertaking a period of study and integration before first degree initiation.

Wiccans also practice other rites of passage. These include namegivings for babies, commonly called "Wiccaning", funerary rites or requiems, and wedding rites which are known as "handfastings".

Taking your First Steps

It can be very daunting when you first start exploring a new subject, and Wicca is no exception. There are a few questions which are often raised by students first starting out, so we thought we would address some of the most commonly asked ones in this section.

Ethics & Wicca

We have a simple ethical code which is expressed in the eight words *"An it harm none, do as ye will"*. This phrase is called the "Wiccan Rede".

Rede is said to be an old word for "council" or "advice", which is exactly what the Wiccan Rede is – it is a philosophical statement which has many possible applications and interpretations.

The Wiccan Rede provides you with a personal guideline which you can use whenever you need to make an important decision. Not just decisions in regard to magickal workings, but also in your every day life. The Wiccan Rede places the emphasis on personal responsibility for all your actions. It says "hold on a minute, do you need to do that? How will your actions affect you? Are you sure you want to go ahead?"

The Wiccan Rede helps us to think about cause and effect, which is an essential part of magickal work. It is up to you to decide whether or not you should proceed. Some people find that the meaning of the words change as they gain in experience.

Furthermore, it is important to keep in mind that hurt and harm are not quite the same thing. If you follow the Wiccan Rede you should strive towards always giving careful consideration to all your actions.

Your Personal Magickal Diary

One of the most important things you should do, right from the beginning is to keep a diary of everything you learn and experience. Keep a note of when and where you performed your ritual or meditation; the time of the day and phase of the moon should also be noted down. In addition you should keep a record of all the techniques you used, invocations, spells and of course the results achieved.

Writing up your rituals, meditations and other magickal experiences forms a very important part of your development and learning, and is one simple, but important ritual in itself, which should not be ignored. If possible you should also write up your dreams, as there is often a great deal to be learned from examining the symbolism of your unconscious mind through examining the visions which come to you in dreamtime.

Looking back over your magickal diaries will show you how you have changed and grown as a person with time and practice, as well as indicating which techniques work best for you.

The Book of Shadows

This term, which is often shorten to *BOS* is used to describe the book of rituals and spells which is traditionally copied by hand by a new initiate. Such books of shadows are said to be *oathbound* which means that they are not to be given or shown to anyone apart from other initiates in the same tradition.

Contrary to what many have claimed, there are many different books of shadows, as each witch is encouraged to add their own rituals and spells to the book they copied from their High Priestess or High Priest. When they in turn pass it on to their own initiates the book may be significantly different from that which they themselves copied, although of course some material will remain the same.

By creating your own magickal journal, as described earlier in this chapter, you are in effect creating your own book of shadows – and if you wish you can name it as such.

Resistance

When you first start performing Wiccan ritual, you will need to practice on a regular basis, as the techniques, like all new skills, will need to be perfected in order for you to become proficient in them.

A common problem, when one first starts practicing ritual, is a feeling of resistance, as the ego naturally reacts against the motions of change. This resistance needs to be overcome in order to practice successful ritual and is a common phenomenon which may recur. The human ego likes a very ordered and rigid existence and through practicing magickal ritual, whether Wiccan or otherwise, you will set the forces of change into motion.

As you overcome this resistance you may start noticing changes in yourself, you may feel more confident, have more energy and feel motivated to explore new horizons. One of the aims of practicing Wicca is the realization of your own potential, through creating a personal understanding of your connection to the web of life all around you. Through overcoming the obstacles which are placed in your way you can realise this potential and strive towards perfection.

Changes

You should be aware that your perceptions will shift as you perform more and more ritual. You will become more sensitive to subtle energies, in ritual, in yourself, in the world around you and in people and their behaviour. This can sometimes cause feelings of isolation, as you find yourself having less in common with people who do not share your interests. You find yourself questioning them and their actions.

There is a pitfall here that must be avoided. Wicca may take you away from friends, as you grow and change, which may be in a very different direction from them. If this happens to you, you need to accept this, and not preach or try and tell them how wonderful, or worse, better, your path is. If Wicca is a path which is right for them, they will find it in their own time, just like you did. Do not try and convince them that your beliefs and experiences are better and do not look down on them for not following the same spiritual path as you.

Best way of Solitary Learning?

This may seem like a trivial question, but it is something that is often asked by those starting out and wishing to work solitary. Our advice would be that you learn from as many sources as possible, by doing this you will find your own way of doing things.

Read as many books as you can find, search for information on the internet, join internet forums where you can interact with others and ask questions, go to public ceremonies if they are available in your area, attend workshops and conferences, do correspondence courses etc. Learn as much as you can about mythology and folklore associated with the place you live in and the cultures you are most interested in.

Most importantly spend time in nature, observe the changing seasons, learn about the trees, the plants, herbs and animal life. Learn to meditate and practice it on a regular basis. And finally, there is no better way of learning than through doing – the only way of being a Wiccan and understanding the rituals and celebrations is to practice and learn through experience.

High Priestess & High Priest

In Wiccan covens, the terms High Priestess and High Priest are used to describe the leaders of the coven. In most traditions, such persons will be second or third degree initiates, who have left the covens which initiated them, to start their own.

The terms are not relevant to solitary practitioners, as they infer a role of responsibility to others. The High Priestess leads a coven of witches, not just in rituals, but also takes responsibility for their training and spiritual welfare. The High Priest assists her with this role, taking an equal role in their training and development, as well as organising rituals and other meetings. In some instances, a coven may have just a High Priestess or just a High Priest.

In some traditions the term is used for all second and third degree initiates, so one coven may have several High Priestesses and High Priests. In such instances, the responsibilities may be shared. We personally use these terms only for people who run their own covens.

Skyclad

Many Wiccans perform their rituals skyclad, which means that rituals are performed in the nude, clad only the light of the stars and moon. There are many reasons given for why this is done. In the Charge of the Goddess it says *"...as a sign that you shall be truly free, you shall be naked in your rites..."*. In this line, which is borrowed from *The Aradia*, by Charles Leland, a personal freedom which is very important to Wiccans is described.

By working skyclad we overcome social conditioning and personal inhibitions, which helps us to attain a freedom of mind and spirit. Some have suggested that it is necessary to work skyclad as clothing may inhibit the flow of energy from the body, we personally feel that if this is the case that it is probably necessary to learn how to raise and direct energy in a manner that clothing does not interfere with it, as it is not always possible to take your clothes off when you need to do a ritual or direct energy.

Skyclad is optional for solitaries, those thinking of working in a coven should inquire about this practice prior to joining a group, some groups work skyclad for all rituals, some work skyclad only for some ceremonies and when the weather permits, where as yet others may work robed for all ceremonies.

In traditional initiatory Wiccan covens, the first degree ceremony is always performed skyclad as it represents a rebirth into the coven and the tradition. Here being skyclad represents both trust between the coven and the new initiate, as well as being symbolic of birth itself. Solitaries performing rites of self-dedication may prefer to do so skyclad for the latter reason.

Meditation & Visualisation

There are two vital skills you need to know and master to really perform effective Wiccan ritual, - meditation and visualisation. These are like the foundations of a house, without them the house is likely to fall down, but with them the house will be strong and can be extended and built higher.

Meditation

Meditation is concentration on a single stimulus, rather than the constant ever-changing stimuli of the world we live in. The stimulus is usually an image or its absence (i.e. a blank wall of colour), or a simple repetitive action, such as chanting or rhythmic breathing.

Meditation calms the mind and stills the spirit, a vital prerequisite for magickal work. By meditating you can shut out everything from the mundane world and focus purely on the magick you are going to perform.

When you begin meditating you will usually find your mind starts to fill with images or events from the day. The preconscious mind floods your conscious mind with distracting details. Irrelevant information like your shopping list or credit card statement may fill your mind. Ignore these and gently push them aside, returning to the stimulus that is the focus of your meditation. This is the first stage, of concentration.

Next your body will try and distract you. You may find yourself feeling sudden itches, or pins and needles, or nagging aches. Ignore these, as this is the ego trying to resist the transformative effect of meditation. When you move past these distractions, you achieve the second stage of meditation, which is serenity.

Now your mind is free to receive intuitions and ideas relating to the symbols or whatever focus you are using for your meditation. This is the third stage of meditation, insight.

At any time during meditation your ego might try a sneak attack, and distract you again with those irrelevant images or body pains. Gently push them away and return to your focus. Do not allow them to irritate you, as they are a natural occurrence, and no reflection on your abilities.

A form of meditation that is commonly used is pathworking, or guided meditation. Pathworkings are meditative journeys used to explore mythic and astral landscapes, to gain insights into myths, spiritual creatures, and yourself. By exploring such landscapes you allow all aspects of your consciousness to communicate, bringing insights and cues from both your unconscious and your higher self.

Pathworkings are often performed in a group context with one person acting as the guide and describing the journey, though they can equally be performed alone.

Visualisation

Visualisation has been described as the process of creating or realising a symbol (or series of symbols) to focus and harness the power of the mind. It is a pictorial rather than a verbal way of thinking. By developing your ability to visualise you train your creative imagination and harness its creative ability.

Visualisation enables you to see symbols, perform pathworkings, visualise the intent of a spell, and perform astral work and psychic work. Some lucky people find they are able to visualise easily and naturally, but for many others it is a skill that needs to be developed. Learning and practising visualisation is like developing a new set of muscles, but mental ones rather than physical ones.

The easiest way to develop your visualisation skills is to practice them every day. Spend some time, say 10-15 minutes, visualising a simple image, like a red triangle for fire, or blue circle for water. Hold this image on a black background. Every time the image changes, be it a change of shape or colour; reform the image so it is back to the original image. Keep practising this until you can hold the image exactly for that 10 or 15 minutes without a single change of colour or shape.

This may take you a while to do, so don't get disheartened if you are still finding it mutating occasionally after a few weeks of practice. When you can hold the image unchanging, your powers of visualisation will be well honed. Even at this point it is still worth practicing to refine your skills.

The Four Elements

Air, Fire, Water and Earth – the four elements which makes up everything, are not just physical, they are also energy states, states of being and philosophical concepts and an integral part of the Wiccan tradition.

In order to understand the symbolism used within ritual and to perform the rituals efficiently it is important to realise how fundamentally important the four elements are to our very existence. They are the building blocks of life and to work effective magick you will need to become familiar with their interaction and presence in the world we live in, in yourself, and to also strive towards a greater understanding of how they work together.

Working with the elements enables us to balance ourselves and remain centred, and promotes growth through realisation of imbalances in ourselves (be they qualities, emotions, habits, etc) and the means to change the imbalances, through working with them and transmuting them.

Whenever you are out in nature the elements are all around you. The air that you breathe also blows past you as wind, the warmth of sun light comes from the fire of our star, water rains on us and is in the rivers, lakes, oceans, etc, and the earth is everywhere, giving form to the land and everything on it.

Meditating in different environments like woods, hilltops, fields, by the sea or rivers, etc, will help you attune to the way the elements surround us and interact with us. Indeed spending a significant period outdoors in as natural an environment as is possible is a good way of reconnecting with nature, and we would recommend doing so on a regular basis.

Air – To Know

Air is the breath of life. We are surrounded by air all the time, invisible yet ever-present. Air is the subtlest of the four elements, intangible and connecting us to the stars, filling the gap between the Earth and the heavens.

Air represents the intellect, the power of thought and knowledge. The magickal axiom for air is *To Know*, reflecting this association with knowledge. With knowledge comes the power of communication to transmit knowledge, best expressed through the words we speak, which travel through the air.

Air is associated with inspiration, a term which can literally mean to breathe in. When we are inspired ideas move in our minds, and movement is a quality of air, as seen in nature by the power of the wind, which can vary from a gentle breeze to a raging tornado. Another quality of Air is clarity, the ability to perceive clearly, analyse the facts and then exercise discernment, i.e. informed choice based on knowledge.

Air is also associated with joy and happiness, the lightness of spirit you feel when you are in a good mood. Feeling happy is often described as "floating on air".

Air Correspondences

Colours	White, Yellow
Time	Dawn, Spring
Direction	East
Gender	Male
Sense	Smell
Tools	Wand, Bailine, Censer
Instruments	Flutes, Pan-Pipes, Wind Instruments
Crystals	Agate, chalcedony, citrine quartz, kunzite, lapis lazuli, opal, sapphire, sodalite, turquoise
Scents	Benzoin, eucalyptus, lavender, pine
Elementals	Sylphs
Archangel	Raphael
Planets	Mercury, Jupiter, Uranus
Zodiacal Signs	Aquarius, Gemini, Libra
Positive Qualities	Analysis, Clarity, Decisiveness, Discernment, Happiness, Hope, Inspiration, Joy, Logic, Wisdom
Negative Qualities	Anxiety, Dispersion, Fear, Impulsiveness, Indecision, Insecurity, Paranoia, Prejudice

Fire – To Will

Fire is the great transformer. Fire is the least obviously present around us on the Earth of the four elements. It is the next most subtle of the elements after air, it flickers and dances, leaping up to die down and be gone again. It is probably for this reason that it is sometimes referred to as the "living element".

Fire can be creative or destructive, and this is clearly seen in nature. A forest fire may initially seem devastating, but many plants actually need fire in their life cycle to ensure their continued survival, a fact that research has made clear in recent years.

Fire burns, and reminds us of the importance of control. When handled properly fire provides light and heat, and can be used to cook and for protection. If allowed to get out of control it can cause great destruction. In the same way fire represents our will and our passions. If controlled they can be creative and constructive, enabling us to develop and do great things. But if we let them get out of control we can become obsessive, or violent.

The magickal axiom associated with fire is *To Will*, reflecting its creative, dynamic and energetic qualities. Through the light of fire we receive illumination, and can see our path, enabling the process of transformation that it facilitates to continue.

Fire is also associated with courage and freedom. To be free we must be brave, and be willing to use our creativity and drive to succeed. Fire motivates us to succeed and refine our passions.

Fire Correspondences

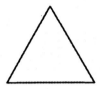

Colours	Orange, Red
Time	Noon, Summer
Direction	South
Gender	Male
Sense	Sight
Tools	Athame
Instruments	Rattles, Sistrums
Crystals	Amber, calcite (orange), garnet, heliotrope, obsidian, ruby, spinel, topaz
Scents	Basil, cinnamon, frankincense, ginger, hyssop, juniper, rosemary
Elementals	Salamanders
Archangel	Michael
Planets	Mars, Sun
Zodiacal Signs	Aries, Leo, Sagittarius
Positive Qualities	Courage, Creativity, Drive, Energy, Freedom, Light, Motivation, Passion, Power, Purification, Success, Transformation, Will
Negative Qualities	Anger, Cruelty, Egotism, Fear, Possessiveness, Vengeance, Violence

Water – To Dare

Life began in the waters. Water is vital for life, and like fire it can be both nurturing and destructive. In nature water is all around us as rain, rivers, lakes and oceans. The seas move in tides, and this reflects our emotions, which ebb and flow like those tides.

The magickal axiom of water is *To Dare*, which we must do if we are to control our emotions and not let them run away with us, like a tidal wave. We must also dare to push the boundaries of our learning and our experience, another important step on any magickal path.

Water can represent both serenity, like the still surface of a lake, or sexual energy and love, which can be as changeable as the sea.

Like air, water transports things, and this is reflected in the associated sense of taste, which tells us whether we want to eat or drink something. Water can be overwhelming, reflecting extremes, from the nurturing it provides to death when it is in its extreme forms.

The dreamlike quality of sun or moon light sparkling on water also indicates another watery association, that of dreams. Our dreams are messages from the depths of our unconscious, rising to the surface of our consciousness like a whale from the deeps.

Water Correspondences

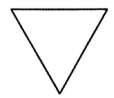

Colours	Blue
Time	Dusk, Autumn
Direction	West
Gender	Female
Sense	Taste
Tools	Chalice
Instruments	Rain Pipes
Crystals	Amethyst, aquamarine, beryl, coral, kyanite, moonstone, pearl, prase, quartz, tourmaline
Scents	Camphor, eucalyptus, geranium, jasmine, lotus, sandalwood, ylang ylang
Elementals	Undines
Archangel	Gabriel
Planets	Moon, Neptune
Zodiacal Signs	Cancer, Pisces, Scorpio
Positive Qualities	Compassion, Death, Dreams, Emotions, Empathy, Intuition, Nurturing, Rebirth, Serenity, Sexuality, Sympathy, Trust
Negative Qualities	Deceit, Hatred, Jealousy, Sorrow, Spite, Treachery

Earth – To Keep Silent

Earth gives us the solidity of the physical which we inhabit. Earth is the most solid of the elements, and hence has associated qualities like endurance, patience, tolerance and steadfastness. Earth is also associated with sensuality, reflected in the pleasures of physical activity.

The sense of touch is associated with earth, we say we are "in touch" with someone when we keep a link between us. The magickal axiom of earth is *To Be Silent*, and this describes the enduring stillness of earth, which can be felt when you go and stand on a mountain or even in a field.

Earth is associated with strength, as it provides the solidity needed to give things their form. Earth is also a nurturing element, providing the food we eat, and making up the materials used to build houses, and indeed being the ground beneath our feet. Earth teaches us that through dedication, patience and toil, all things are possible.

Earth also emphasises selflessness and responsibility. To live in a pleasant physical environment we must act responsibly and in community with others, being heard when we speak out for our environment.

Earth Correspondences

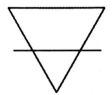

Colours	Brown, Green
Time	Midnight, Winter
Direction	North
Gender	Female
Sense	Touch
Tools	Pentacle
Instruments	Drums, Percussion Instruments
Crystals	Amber, aventurine, chrysocolla, emerald, fluorite, jadeite, jet, magnetite, malachite, nephrite, onyx, smoky quartz, staurolite, zoisite
Scents	Cedar, myrrh, patchouli, pine, vetivert
Elementals	Gnomes
Archangel	Uriel
Planets	Pluto, Saturn, Venus
Zodiacal Signs	Capricorn, Taurus, Virgo
Positive Qualities	Endurance, Humility, Patience, Responsibility, Selflessness, Sensuality, Steadfastness, Stillness, Strength, Tolerance
Negative Qualities	Attention-Seeking, Depression, Domineering, Greed, Inertia, Laziness, Melancholy, Stubbornness

Spirit – To Go or Become

Spirit is the most intangible of the elements, existing when the other four elements are in balance. Spirit represents the creative essence of growth and reproduction that permeates all life. It is the divine spark or soul that resides in all of us and joins us together.

The web of existence unites all life in the element of spirit. Spirit gives us the impetus to grow, to transcend our limits and realise our own potential, to discover our talents and use them.

Spirit is also connected with the psychic senses, which are a way of receiving the subtle energies which flow through the web of existence between us all. The more "spiritual" a person becomes, the more in tune with their environment they become.

The magickal axiom of spirit is *To Go* or *To Become*, indicating the sense of evolutionary movement connected with spirit. The going refers to the magickal journey of self-discovery, not purely physical movement. After all you can become more aware through sitting and quietly meditating.

Spirit Correspondences

Colours	Black, Purple, White
Time	Outside of Time
Direction	Within/Without
Gender	Both
Sense	Hearing
Tools	Bell, Cauldron, Sword
Instruments	Voice
Crystals	Amethyst, diamond, kunzite, jadeite, labradorite, opal, pearl, sapphire, tourmaline, zircon
Scents	Frankincense, lotus
Elementals	-
Archangel	Metatron
Planets	-
Zodiacal Signs	-
Positive Qualities	Evolution, Harmony, Life Force, Sixth Sense, Transcendence, Transformation
Negative Qualities	None

Elemental Body Meditation

The elements are all present within us, in our bodies and in our souls. Meditating on the elements within your body can help you gain a deeper appreciation of how the elements work, and your relationship with them.

Sit and quietly meditate. Start by focusing on the air entering and leaving your body through your nostrils and/or mouth as you breathe. Be aware of the air passing down your throat and into your lungs. From here concentrate on the oxygen, passing through the walls of the lungs into your blood stream, and being transported all through your body, to all your cells, to help them function. Be aware of the space within your body as well, the space in your mouth and nose that is filled with air, and in your throat and lungs. Now focus on the breath leaving your body, the carbon dioxide and water that the body is getting rid of as waste products. Air communicates and moves things, and you can feel this in your body.

Now move your attention to the element of fire within your body. Think about all the nerve impulses, synapses firing electrical signals that are sending messages round your body all the time, and keeping it functioning automatically. Concentrate as well on the fire of digestion going on in your stomach, as food is transformed into useable components to sustain your body and keep it alive. Feel the transforming and quickening power of fire within you.

Next move your attention to water. Water makes up around 80% of your body. Be aware of water as the blood flowing through your arteries and veins, as the saliva in your mouth, the moisture in your eyes, and the contents of most of your cells, the fluid within the cells that comprises them. Water sustains you, and moves the flow of energy around your body.

Bring your awareness to earth. Earth provides the solidity of form that makes your body what it is. Earth gives form to your bones and your muscles, your nails, teeth, hair and skin. Earth is the solid binding force that keeps the elements in you connected and connects you to the Earth you live on.

Finally move your awareness to spirit. Spirit comes into being when the other four elements are in harmony, as they are in your body. Spirit is the spark of life within you, your soul, your mind, your intuition, your emotions, your personality, indeed all the subtle and intangible qualities that define you as a person.

Consider how all the elements are present within you, and how their interaction makes you the person you are, defining your body and your spirit. Remember that you too are a being of the elements. Bring your awareness back to your breathing for a few breaths, and then record your impressions.

The Goddess & God

Wiccans share a belief in both a Goddess and God, a feminine and masculine divine. This belief is rooted in the beliefs of ancient cultures, where there were many female as well as male deities.

In Wicca, the Goddess and God are celebrated at each of the seasonal festivals and are called upon in rites of devotion and magick throughout the year.

In some Wiccan traditions, a specific Goddess and God are chosen as the tutelary deities and a Coven or individual may work with just those deities. Popular deities amongst Wiccans include the Goddesses Aradia, Diana, Artemis, Hekate, The Morrigan, Ceridwen, Arianrhod, Bride and the Gods Cernunnos, Pan, Hades, Gwyn Ap Nudd, Hermes, Herne, Apollo.

In some instances, a person or group may work with Goddesses and Gods other than their tutelary deities, or they may work with a specific pantheon only. Some refer to the Goddess and God as Lord and Lady or simply as "Goddess" and "God" rather than naming them.

The Goddess is seen as being omnipresent and immortal, and in Wicca she is often seen as primarily associated with the Moon, but also with the Stars, the Earth and the Underworld. She is viewed as the Creatrix who gave birth to the God, and then joined with him in sacred union to create the universe.

Stellar aspects like the Celtic Arianhrod, Egyptian Nuit and Greek Nox are representative of the Goddess as the totality of all life, containing all within her body. As the Lunar Goddess, in aspects like the Greek Artemis and Selene and Roman Diana, she represents the changing ebbs and flows of life, symbolised by the phases of the Moon.

As the Earth Goddess, like the Greek Gaia and Demeter, Roman Ceres and Celtic Ceridwen, she represents the fertility of nature and the Earth. As the Underworld Goddess, like the Greek Persephone and Hekate, and the Sumerian Ereshkigal, she represents the transformation of death and rebirth, like a seed rising anew from the ground.

The God is often seen in three main aspects in Wicca – as the Horned God of the Wildwood, the Sun King, and the Dread Lord of Shadows. The God is the consort of the Goddess, her lover and son who dies and is reborn through her love on a yearly basis as experienced through the changing seasons of nature.

The God is seen by some people as being less important than the Goddess. However it is important to remember that Wicca is about balance, and this includes the polarity and balance of energies between Goddess & God, Feminine & Masculine.

The God in his aspects emphasises the positive masculine qualities, and can help people overcome negative stereotypes of the masculine and masculine divine that they may bring with them from previous religious and social conditioning.

As the Horned God, he represents the wildness of nature, the fertilising power of conscious action. Gods like the Celtic Cernunnos, Herne and Gwyn Ap Nudd, and the Greek Pan, embody this aspect.

As the Sun God, like the Greek Helios and Apollo, the Roman Sol and Celtic Belenus, he represents the illuminating and life-giving rays of the sun.

The Dread Lord of Shadows, God of Death and Resurrection, is the comforter and transformer who guides the soul through the stages of change. He is represented by Gods like the Greek Hades, Egyptian Osiris, and Celtic Gwyn Ap Nudd.

Practitioners hold individual views on the nature of the Goddess and God, as there is no one prescribed view. Wiccans may be polytheistic, duotheistic, henotheistic, animistic, pantheistic – or even a combination of the aforementioned.

The Old Ones

The Old Ones, sometimes called the *Timeless Ones* or *Forgotten Ones*, are an integral part of the web of forces that permeate nature. The term *Old Ones* is used to collectively describe a whole range of beings. It includes our ancestors, the faery folk, genius loci ("spirits of places") and site guardians, and indwelling nature spirits such as dryads and hamadryads (from trees) and nymphs (from pools and rivers).

The practice of working with the Old Ones originates with traditional forms of witchcraft, but many Wiccans have also incorporated it into their rituals. The Old Ones can be seen as representing the wild and free aspect of Wicca, the pleasure of the dance under the silver moon, connecting us to the land and our ancestors, who have gone before us.

The Old Ones can serve as a gateway into the more subtle aspects of nature, helping one to deepen appreciation and understanding of the wilderness. The Old Ones bring with them a sense of freedom and creativity that can fill the circle like a spring breeze fresh with the scent of May blossoms. They inspire poetry, music and dance, and help you to break free of your social self and be part of the natural world, flowing with the tides and the breezes of the earth, sea and sky.

We always invoke the Old Ones when we work outdoors, and make offerings in their honour during the ceremony of cakes and wine. We invoke them before we invoke the Goddess and God, as we view it as courteous to include the beings whose space we are in. Likewise, we thank and bid them farewell after we have done so for the Goddess and God.

To really appreciate the Old Ones and the wide range of forces they embody, you should try working with them at a whole range of sites that include different environments, such as woodlands, lakes, mountains, seashore, stone circles or burial chambers, etc. You can even make them the focus of your ritual and perform workings with just the Old Ones without calling to the Goddess and God.

Example Invocation to the Old Ones:

Hail Old Ones,
Ancient Ones of Time and Space
You who were before the first breath
You who will be after the last ember
Hail indwelling spirits of tree and rock and lake
Hail dryads, nymphs and fairies,
Hail guardians of sacred sites
Hail ancestors,
You who have walked these paths before us
And whose wisdom flows in our veins
Join me now! Hail to thee!

Wiccan Ritual

Wiccan ritual as we know it today originated from rituals which were popularized and developed by Gerald B. Gardner during the late 1940's and the 1950's, with the help of priestesses such as Doreen Valiente.

The result of his work, and that of other people who followed during the 1960's and 1970's, such as Alex & Maxine Sanders, is the structure we have today for working ritual which is used by covens, individuals and many other neo-pagan groups the world over. In addition to its use within Wiccan covens and traditions, we have seen it used by Egyptian revivalists groups, feminist groups, Fellowship of Isis Lyceums, Druids and even Chaos magicians!

Ritual has been called the technology of the sacred and just like other technologies constantly changes to adapt to its circumstances, so the rituals within traditions have been undergoing constant evolution with each individual or group who practiced them. Today there are very few groups who adhere strictly to the rituals as presented by Gerald Gardner to his own covens, instead each individual adds to and changes the rituals to suit their own personal needs.

For this very reason no two covens are ever exactly alike and even within the same tradition there can be many significant differences. The personalities, energies and interests of the individuals within a group will ensure that no two rituals are the same, even if two groups perform exactly the same ritual.

Whenever you are working magick, you need to understand what you are doing and why you are doing it, and pay attention to what works and what doesn't work for you. In this way you can ensure that you are spiralling upwards, rather than diminishing what is a really great system already.

Once you understand the symbolism and techniques, it becomes easy to adapt rituals to suit your own needs and tastes. But to come to that understanding, you will first need to learn and practice the rituals, a process which may take some time. Unless you understand the symbolism and purpose of each ritual component, you are not qualified to decide that any part of a ritual is obsolete or unnecessary. Doing so would be like driving a car with two flat tyres – it might move and it might even continue to do so for a while – but it is certainly not desirable! Of course there are ritual components which can be adapted, changed, omitted, added to and more, but first make sure that you understand the reasons for it being there in the first place, before doing so.

When you are first starting out, do things the *tried and tested* way, this may be the way you are taught by a teacher or a group, or what you learn from books. Consider carefully the symbolism and purpose of each small detail of the ritual, and make sure that you understand it. Once you reach that point, it should be easy to adapt it to your own likes and needs, and to indeed write wholly individual, creative, inspiring and unique rituals.

In our own covens we often perform freeform work with great success, but each and every member of the Coven is first taught the traditional forms of the rituals and expected to be fluent in them.

By taking this approach, you can decide what suits you best – as you have experienced more than one way of practising the different ritual components. Additionally you can adapt and write your own original rituals with a thorough understanding and experience of magickal symbolism, rather than writing rituals which are empty forms which seem to be impressive, with words and symbolism which are meaningless!

Wiccan ritual consists of a basic structure. There is a formal opening, a formal closing and certain activities which are performed at nearly every ritual. Within that structure there is scope for a lot of freedom and creative expression, both for groups and individuals.

Wiccan ritual is in no way dogmatic, nor is it a liturgy. However it does follow a set pattern of working, which is what defines it as being Wiccan ritual, rather than that of a different tradition. There are no restrictions on how you should and should not perform your rituals - the only limitations are your own understanding, knowledge and personal creative interpretation of the rituals, their purpose and their symbolism.

Wiccan Ritual Structure:

* Preparation of the ritual space
* Preparation and purification of the participants
* Purification of the ritual space
* Casting the magick circle
* Invocation of the Quarter Guardians
* Invocation of the Goddess
* Invocation of the God
* Magickal workings – devotion, divination, healing, spells etc.
* Cakes & Wine
* Rite of departure for the God
* Rite of departure for the Goddess
* Banishing the Guardians of the Four Quarters
* Opening the Circle

Wicca was designed as a ritual tradition – i.e. through the practice of certain rituals we achieve mystical states and they can trigger direct experiences of the Divine. All the tools, symbols, actions, words and thoughts that you use in ritual have a purpose. That purpose is to focus your will to precisely and effectively direct your intent towards achieving the aim of the ritual.

The ritual structure may at first seem restrictive and formulaic, but it is exactly the opposite. By using the same method for creating sacred space at each of our ceremonies, we build on our experience and knowledge of the ritual and symbolism used, as we gain in experience. Furthermore, it places the focus back on the content of the ritual, rather than the creation of the sacred space itself, which allows us to spend more time and energy on our relationship with deity, learning and experience and results.

It is for this reason that it is very important that the first step in preparing for your ritual is to clarify what the purpose of your ritual is. Ritual is a very powerful experience, as it helps restore a sense of the sacred, and acts as a gateway between the physical mundane world we live our lives in, and the subtle unseen worlds of the Gods and spiritual beings. So when you have the powerful experience that ritual can generate, it helps greatly if you have a clear focus.

Circle of Fire

There is no point in expending energy in a ritual that you perform just for the sake of it. Consider what you are trying to achieve – will it be a celebrational ritual to mark the changing seasons, a devotional ritual, or a spell for a specific result or are you performing this ritual with the intent of performing a divination? Or indeed a combination of more than one of these components?

Having a clear intent for each ritual you perform will help you gain deeper insights and give you a feeling of accomplishment once you have achieved the goals you have set for yourself.

It is important to be precise in your wording of a ritual, as well as the symbolism that you include. Precision does not necessarily mean that you need to say everything word perfect, it does however mean that you need to know what it is that you say and that there are no ambiguities. The Gods tend to have a sense of humour when it comes to these things and the saying "be careful what you wish for, you may just get it" is a common phrase amongst Witches, especially those who have experienced it first hand! The same is true for symbolism, try and make sure that you are not confusing the goals you set yourself, by using inappropriate correspondences!

The magick that you do, be it a spell or otherwise, will put forces of change into motion, changes which will affect you. Make sure that you are both willing and able to accept those changes and the effects that they will bring and make sure that you consider all possible outcomes before you perform your magick. You may desire certain changes to your life, but make sure that you are ready for those changes when they happen!

Ritual Tools

There are many tools which may be used in Wiccan ritual. The most frequently used of the standard tools are those which correspond to the elements. These are the athame (fire), wand (air), chalice (water) and pentacle (earth). Additionally the other standard tools are the censer (air), scourge (fire), cords, bailine (air) and sword (spirit).

Tools are used to focus the energies of a ritual in a particular way, appropriate to that moment in the ritual. Hence the sword, athame or wand, which are directing tools, are used for casting the circle, whereas the pentacle, which is a receiving tool, is used as the basis for consecrations, and the chalice, another receiving tool, to hold the wine.

As well as being functional, tools are also symbolic and understanding their symbolism can make your rituals richer and more rewarding. Not understanding the symbolism of a tool may lead to you misinterpreting the rituals and not understanding the rituals that you work.

One way to appreciate the symbolism of your tools is to meditate on them before using them. This also has the added benefit of attuning you to each of your tools, making them feel like familiar friends, or even extensions of yourself. You should meditate on each tool in turn, so that you have done this for all of them.

Hold the tool in your hand, and contemplate it. Consider its shape, what it is made of, what you will use it for, and what it symbolises. Close your eyes and spend time just feeling the energy of the tool. What impressions do you get from it? How do you feel holding it? Do this as many times as you wish until you feel you have a clear grasp of the tool's nature, and feel strongly attuned to it.

We will consider the use and symbolism of each of the ritual tools in turn, including other commonly used tools which are not always discussed, as they are not considered "traditional" by some.

The Athame or Black Handled Dagger

The traditional athame is a black handled dagger, usually with a double-edged blade. It is sometimes also referred to as the black handled knife, although today there are many wonderful designs available which means that some traditions and solitary practitioners might choose designs with different coloured handles and ornately shaped blades.

The athame is often described as "the real witch's weapon", which is a good description as it represents the personal power of the individual, the power of the mind, the focus and discrimination.

The term "weapon" is used here to indicate its function in creating the protective circle and drawing the pentagrams at the four cardinal points to further aid in the protection and empowerment of the magick circle.

The athame is generally taken to represent the element of Fire, although some traditions ascribe it to the element of Air instead. The argument for the athame being attributed to fire is that it has a steel blade, which is forged in fire, and it represents the will of the individual, which is also associated with the element of fire.

The athame represents the will of the individual witch who wields it. In ritual the athame is an active weapon to be wielded. It is often used for casting the circle, especially in circumstances where you do not have the space or where it is not practical to wield a sword, or when working solitary.

The athame is also used for consecrations. It is most often used to consecrate the salt and water for purifying the space, as well as the cakes and wine at the end of the ceremony.

The athame represents the male principle during the symbolic Great Rite when the wine is consecrated by the Priest and Priestess. The athame is never used to cut anything, and should never be used to draw blood. This is because the athame can be seen as an extension of the will of the wielder, and you are using an athame to direct energy, not to cause harm.

The Bailine (Boline)

The bailine is sometimes called the white-handled knife and is a functional tool. The bailine is often shown resembling a small sickle, but this is extremely impractical for its actual uses, and realistically the bailine should be a practical knife that you can cut and etch with. The bailine is traditionally a white-handled knife, although many people today may choose a different coloured handle according to their personal preference.

The bailine, like the wand, is considered to represent the element of Air. As with the athame, the use of the bailine also stem from the *Key of Solomon*, a fact acknowledged by Gerald Gardner in his book, *High Magic's Aid*:

> *"Thur recited anew those same Psalms of David, then, throwing the herbs on the brazier, he waited until the clouds of incense ascended, and took up an engraver's awl. He purified it on the live coals and, with the white-handled knife, whose office was that of a tool as distinct from that of the Athame used by the witch to control spirits and work magic, he carved on the handle of the awl, which was to become the Burin, these characters."* [1]

The bailine is used within the circle to etch or carve sigils and symbols into items such as candles or wands. It is also used to carve wands and help with the making of other tools. Another practical use of the bailine is to cut food.

---

[1] *High Magic's Aid* – Gerald Gardner, p100, 1949.

The Sword

The sword can also represent the will of the wielder and is used to direct and command energy. During a Wiccan ceremony there will usually only be one sword in the circle, wielded by either the High Priest or High Priestess. When used within a coven ritual it represents the combined will and goals of the group.

The sword symbolises Spirit, as the active will of the wielder or group. Some people attribute it to fire because of the forging process, but this ignores the difference in scale between the sword and the other elemental tools, and also the association of the sword with nobility and authority. The sword was the standard weapon borne by the angels and archangels, sometimes in conjunction with a pair of scales to show balance and divine justice.

The sword is used to cast the circle and to direct power. In Handfasting ceremonies it is sometimes used to cut the cake.

The Wand

The wand is used to direct energy in a similar manner to the athame. The wand is representative of the element of Air (some people use it for the element of fire due to the attribution in the Tarot), representing the life-force and healing (hence the caduceus). Wands come in many shapes and sizes.

It is traditional for a witch to make their own wand from the wood of a fruit bearing tree. This is classically hazel, representing wisdom and the Moon, although it can be interesting to work with wands made from different woods, corresponding to different elements and energies.

So for instance a wand made from willow could be used to represent watery and healing energies, or a wand made from oak to represent the element of earth and strength, etc. Wands can also be made from crystal or metal and can be engraved or otherwise decorated with symbols and sigils appropriate to the intended use.

Instructions are given regarding wands in the *Key of Solomon*:
> *"...the Wand of hazel or nut tree, in all cases the wood being virgin, that is of one year's growth only. They should each be cut from the tree at a single stroke, on the day of Mercury, at Sunrise."*

The wand can be used for any purpose that the athame is used for, such as casting the circle, drawing invoking and banishing pentagrams, consecrating salt and water or cakes and wine.

One significant consideration with the wand is that is especially appropriate for outdoor workings. Many spirits in nature, such as the faery and site guardians, are thought to not like iron, and so as a mark of respect wooden (or crystal) wands are used in place of athames when working outdoors.

The Chalice

The chalice is used to hold wine, water or any other drink during ritual. Chalices come in many sizes and designs, using a silver one is particularly appropriate if you work with the Moon and is as such the popular choice for Wiccans (however avoid putting fruit juices in metal chalices as it can have an acidic effect and make it taste unpleasant). You can however choose a design that suits your own needs and decorate it to your own tastes. Wood, ceramics and animal horn are all popular alternative choices for chalices.

The chalice represents the element of Water. It is also symbolic of the womb of the Mother Goddess and as such of the receptive feminine principle. The use of cups to hold libations to the Gods is very ancient, the Egyptians, Greek and Romans all used them for this purpose.

The chalice has one main function, which is to hold the drink for the end of the ceremony. It can be used to pour libations as well as to drink from. It can also be used to hold water for ceremonies in which there is an emphasis on the four elements.

The Pentacle

The pentacle is one of the most important tools in Wicca, and is seldom used to its full potential. As the symbol of earth and the base for consecrations, the pentacle can be seen as a mini-altar.

Confusion in terminology has resulted in a number of books referring to the pentagram as the pentacle. This is not the case – a pentagram is a five-pointed star, and a pentacle is a ritual tool. Leading to further confusion is the fact that a pentacle may have the symbol of the pentagram engraved or painted on it.

The pentacle is symbolic of the solidity and endurance of earth and represents the element of Earth in ritual. It is often inscribed with a pentagram and symbols particular to the tradition it is being used in, when working solitary you can decide on the design yourself. There are many craftspeople creating beautiful designs which might suit your needs, you can of course also design and make one yourself.

Some groups use a design with a pentagram representing man (the microcosm) on the front and a hexagram, representing the universe (the macrocosm) on the reverse. This also emphasises the primary magickal axiom *"As Above, So Below"*, which refers to the interconnectedness of all life. The pentacle is usually made from wood, wax or copper, although you can also use a flat stone, crystal or clay, or any other natural material.

The use of pentacles in Wicca was most probably inspired by the pentacles which were made for a variety of reasons by medieval magicians.

The pentacle is the object on which consecrations are performed for ritual tools and spell ingredients. It is often used as a platter for the cakes or bread which are blessed during the ceremony of cakes and wine. The pentacle is also used for wealth spells as it represents the fecundity of the element of earth (think of coins and you get the idea).

The Cords

The cords have a number of uses and symbolisms attached to them. Many Wiccans choose to work with three cords in colours which are symbolic of the principles of life, death and rebirth. Others use cords to represent the different elemental or planetary energies, or of course choose a cord to represent the intent of their spell or ritual.

The use of cord and knot magick was common amongst the magickal practitioners or Ancient Greece and Egypt. Knotted red threads were frequently used in magick.

The cords are used in Wiccan ceremony for binding (being "properly prepared" in a Witches circle). Additionally they are also used for cord magick, spells and to mark the magick circle with.

Wiccans again seem to have borrowed the marking of the circle with a cord from the *Key of Solomon* in which the magician is instructed:
> *"then take a cord of nine feet in length, fasten one end thereof unto the Sickle and with the other end trace out the circumference of the Circle, which may be marked either with the Sword or with the Knife with the Black hilt."*

They may also be worn around your robe or waist during ritual. The three cords are sometimes plaited together to make a cingulum which is worn around the waist during ceremonies and can be useful to hang your athame or other objects from.

Wiccan groups often work with three colours, representing energies that are special to them. This varies between groups – the alchemical colours – white, red and green are quite common, though blue or black in place of green are also common. The three cords can represent many things, such as life, death and rebirth, the Triple Goddess, or the Goddess and Horned God with the Child of Promise.

The Censer

The stimulatory properties of smell in ritual should not be ignored, as smell is one of the strongest prompts to the unconscious available. The censer to hold the stimulating incense can be an ornate object designed for the purpose, or any fireproof dish filled with some clean earth.

The censer represents the element of Air. The use of incense is probably as old as mankind itself. We know that it was very popular amongst the ancient Egyptians, who used it to mark the journey of the Sun God Ra through the day.

The censer holds the incense and enables you to purify a space with incense. Sweet smelling incense is considered to generate a positive atmosphere pleasing to the Gods and spirits, and also purifies the environment you work in. If you are working indoors, using incense helps your mind make the distinction that you are travelling from the mundane to the magickal.

Incense can be used for a wide range of purposes, including focusing the mind, as an act of devotion (using fragrances sacred to specific deities), and for its healing and relaxing effects. It also makes a good medium for skrying in and on practical level can keep distracting insects away when you are outdoors.

To use a censer you will need self-igniting charcoal and loose grain incense. The charcoal should be lit and placed in the container, and the grains of incense burned upon it. Some people prefer to use incense cones or joss sticks instead of loose incense in ritual, it is best to try and experiment with both so that you can choose that which suits your own needs, likes and dislikes best!

If you are going to move the censer during ritual, such as to cense the circle or offer incense at the quarters, remember that hot metal burns, and this is why earth or sand are usually placed in censers to dissipate heat and enable them to be handled.

The Scourge

The scourge is a symbol of dominion and power, which is used more often in group ceremonies than in solitary practice.

The scourge used in Wicca traditionally has eight strands with five knots in each. The eight strands can be said to represent the eight festivals of the Wheel of the Year, as well as the other eight main tools. Five is the number of points on the pentagram, representing the four elements plus spirit. Combining these numbers gives forty knots, a significant number during initiation.

The scourge is held by the High Priestess during Drawing Down the Moon, and represents the Qabalistic Pillar of Severity which is feminine, as opposed to the Pillar of Mercy (represented by the wand), which is masculine.

It is also used, in some traditions, during the initiation ceremony as a symbolic representation of *"art thou willing to suffer to learn"* which is a phrase central to all who follow Wicca as their chosen path. This certainly doesn't mean that we have to all go through life in pain, but instead it warns that to follow a magickal path is not easy or a soft option. It will come with obstacles, your ideals and beliefs will be challenged, you will have to remain open minded at all times and be able to accept the changes that the practice of magick will bring to you.

The Besom

The most stereotypical witch's item! The besom is a purifying tool, and is one of those tools that anyone can make, even if not very practically minded. The besom or broom represents the union of the Goddess, the brush being her yoni, and the God, the rod being his lingam.

Of course we know that witches are supposed to fly on broomsticks, but much earlier than this still, the ancient Egyptians used it to sweep ritual space prior to performing any ritual, in a very similar way that we do today.

The besom is used to symbolically and physically sweep the circle space prior to ritual. It is usually made from ash, birch or broom.

Another popular use of the besom is at Handfasting ceremonies. Handfasting (pagan wedding) ceremonies usually climax with the couple having to jump over the besom for fertility and good luck. If either of them touches the besom when they jump it, the ritual is said to be negated.

The besom is also the tool which was said to have been used to apply the Witches flying ointment to the sensitive parts of the body which eased the absorption of the psychoactive ingredients of the ointment that promoted "spirit flight". However this practice is not one generally used today due to the poisonous and potentially fatal nature of many of the ingredients of such flying ointments.

The Cauldron

The cauldron is the other favourite stereotypical witch's tool. The use of the cauldron as a symbol of witchcraft probably originates from the archetypal image of a witch as an old woman living by herself and cooking up potions in her cauldron (which would have been quite normal as a cooking pot for most people!). However cauldrons seem to be used as religious focus much earlier, an example is the Gundestrup cauldron on which the famous image of Cernunnos appears.

The cauldron represents all the elements and often is as such used in ceremony to represent Spirit. It is a symbol of the Goddess and represents the life giving force of her womb. Spirit is the place where all the elements are formed and where they all return to. The cauldron appears in many myths as a symbol of wisdom, rebirth and of plenty.

The cauldron has a variety of ways it can be put to use in ritual. We often place a small metal bowl inside it with flammable oils which we light at the fire festivals. You can also skry into the flames when using it in this manner. Sometimes we fill the cauldron with water and herbs which we use to bless the circle with, or again to skry into.

The cauldron can be used for spells and as a symbolic representation of the Goddess on the altar, especially appropriate if you work with the Celtic Goddess Ceridwen!

Other Tools

The Bell

The bell is not often found in the list of tools, but it is an item that can be used to great effect in ceremony and is used in initiation rituals. The bell is attributed to Spirit and represents the Vault of Heaven. The chime of the bell represents purity, and is also said to be pleasing to spirits, being particularly popular with the faery folk.

The bell is used to mark points during ritual. It can also be used to great effect during group meditations. The bell is sometimes used in Samhain rituals to call in the spirits of the ancestors for the Feast of the Dead.

The Drum

Although the drum is not specifically a Wiccan tool, it is frequently used within Wicca and needs to be considered. The drum is usually seen as a tool of the element of Earth. The beat of the drum is analogous to the "heartbeat of the Earth". In shamanic cultures the drum is often taken as representing the earth itself, and is in this manner akin to the pentacle.

The drum can be used in a number of ways. You can use a drum to cleanse your space, for dancing and chanting, for trance work, or to raise energy for spells.

An important thing to remember though is the effect of drumming on your environment. If you are working indoors it might upset your neighbours! If you are outdoors in the wilds of nature, remember that late-night drumming sessions can seriously upset the local wildlife, not to mention farmers whose livestock may become distressed.

Robes

Although many Wiccan groups work skyclad, some prefer to wear robes at least some of the time (especially during the colder months!). It is preferable to have robes made of natural fabrics such as wool, cotton or silk. Wool is particularly good for outdoors, to keep the cold out, whereas a light fabric like cotton or silk is better for indoor use.

Wiccan robes today are often based on the robes used by ceremonial traditions, such as the simple Tau, or on renaissance and medieval clothing. Whichever style you decide on working in, remember to keep it practical and comfortable, especially if your ritual involves movement, such as dance.

Robes are worn to represent the change into the magickal personality prior to ritual, when we change out of our everyday clothes and into a robe to perform ritual. As such, wearing them helps to encourage a change in consciousness, which enables us to move more easily from the world of the mundane into the magickal.

Robes can be bought in many colours and designs and if you work solitary you can choose the colour and design you want. Many groups work with black or white robes as standard, and others may use different colours to signify different positions in the group or allow members to wear whichever colour they prefer! If you are working solitary, you may want to choose a colour that you feel a special affinity with, or which is associated with the Goddess or God you work with most.

The Stang

Another tool that is not strictly Wiccan, the stang is nonetheless a popular tool for outdoor work, and has the added bonus of being useable as a (large) walking stick.

The stang was made popular in modern times by Robert Cochrane, the founder of the 1734 tradition. The two points at the top of the stang represent the horns of the Horned God. The three-way connection of the two points with the length of the stang can also be seen as representing the three-way crossroads of Hekate, the ancient Greek Goddess of Witches.

The stang is used for outdoor work in place of the sword, being less obtrusive and also like the wand has the benefit of not containing iron and so is preferable for working in nature. A stang is usually ideally the same height as the person who bears it, which can make finding the right piece of wood challenging at times. The choice of wood for making your stang is a personal preference.

The stang is also sometimes used in spells, such as the cord and stang spell, and as a symbol of the World Tree, placed in the centre of the circle as the axis mundi.

The Salt & Water Bowls

Although not often mentioned as a tool, bowls to hold your salt and water in are an essential item. The bowls can be as simple or complex as you like, or some groups even use shells. The bowls do not need to be very large, and if you are going to use them outdoors it is a good idea to not have bowls made of something fragile.

We use a blue glass bowl for water and a carved wooden bowl for salt. This adds an additional level of symbolism, which adds to the energy and the ambience of the ritual.

Candlesticks

Another essential item often left off lists is candlesticks. Candlesticks can be as ornate or simple as your preference dictates. It is preferable to have a matching pair of candlesticks for your Goddess and God candles on the altar, and you will want at least one other candlestick for your Spirit candle (or four more if you wish to have candles at the quarters for the elements).

PART II – Preparations

Ritual Space

Making every step of the preparation a sacred act will help prepare you for the ritual and enhance your rituals greatly. The preparation should never be a chore, it should be a pleasure!

After you have decided to do a ritual and why you want to do it, you will need to decide where you will go to perform your ritual.

Indoors is the practical option for many of us who live in cities as it provides more privacy and security than working in most city parks. There are of course exceptions and if you spend some time getting to know your local area you may find an outdoor space which is suitable.

Private indoor spaces are convenient for spells, but you may want to work outside for rituals in which you celebrate the changing seasons. There might be a place you can go to which is sacred to the deity you will be working with, or it may be appropriate for you to be near water, on a hill, or even under a specific type of tree.

Indoors or outdoors, near or far from home, you will need to spend time preparing the physical space before the start of your work.

Indoors preparation includes dusting, vacuuming and general tidying, prior to starting the process of setting up for your ritual. A clean and tidy space will also help remove additional distractions which may interfere with your concentration.

If you decide to work outdoors, you should spend some time at the site prior to your ritual in meditation to contact the spirits of the place and obtain their permission to work there. This is an important step, as nature spirits can often cause havoc if they feel that their space is being invaded by unwelcome guests.

We have found that nature spirits appreciate offerings, such as fruits, nuts, milk and honey. It is also a good idea to spend some time clearing the space of any litter and other debris – you should aim to leave a site in as good or in a better condition than you found it. These simple considerations demonstrate your respect to the spirits of the place you are working at.

Also, remember that it might be necessary to sometimes adapt the way in which you work to the place in which you decide to work. If, for example, you find yourself working in a space which has a lake on the south side of your circle, you may want to adapt your ritual by calling the Guardian of Water in the south, rather than in its usual place of the West.

Remember that you will be welcoming spiritual beings such as Goddesses and Gods into your circle, and you should thus prepare the space appropriately.

Planning Your Ritual

Having decided on the purpose of your ritual, the timing and location, you need to get down to the basics of creating your ritual structure. Try sitting down with a pen and paper to write down ideas and thoughts to the following considerations:

Which techniques will you use?

This is a crucial consideration. If you are performing a spell, what type of spell will work best? Should you do a candle spell, and if so should it be a single spell, or a multi-day spell that you do over a period of time? Perhaps a cord and knot spell would be better, or an amulet or talisman.

Having decided on the focus for your spell, you then need to decide what techniques you will use to energise the spell. This is largely down to personal preference as to what works best for you. You may like prolonged periods of chanting to raise energy, or dancing around forming a cone of power, or simply concentrating your intent silently, or another technique. Or you may decide to use more than one technique to generate the energy that will power your spell.

Which Deities will you work with?

In Wicca we call upon both the Goddess and God in our ceremonies, some traditions always work with the same Goddess and God, whereas others are more eclectic and work with a variety of deities. If you are working as a solitary you can try working with a variety of deities, by doing this you will eventually find what works for you. If you are working with a Goddess or God for the first time, make sure to do some research to find out as much as you can about them prior to the ceremony. This will help you attune to their energies, prepare your invocations and of course it is a good way of learning more about the world pantheons. Having decided on which deities to work with, you can include symbolic representations of them on your altar, and prepare appropriate offerings.

What do you need for your ritual?

It's a good idea to make a check list of everything you will need for a specific ritual in advance. This is even more important if you are working outdoors or away from home, as it will avoid a last minute panic when you realise you forgot something which may be integral to your ritual.

Some items may have to be specially prepared or made in advance. If you have a creative streak you may want to, for instance, make your own incense, candles, robes, altar cloths or other altar decorations.

A typical check list may include:

★ The ritual tools you will use – such as a wand, athame, sword, boline, pentacle, chalice, censer, candle sticks, salt & water bowl etc.

In addition you will need:
★ Wine & Cakes for the sacrament
★ Salt & Water for the purification of the space
★ Incense and charcoal blocks (or alternatively joss or smudge sticks).
★ Matches or lighter for lighting the charcoal and candles
★ Anointing oil (if used)
★ Candles (for the altar & spell work)
★ Clean robe (if working robed)
★ Your magickal journal and a pen, for writing up your experiences.
★ Ingredients for any other workings, such as spells or devotions.

If you are taking a bottle of wine, make sure that you have packed the corkscrew, and remember to prepare some food and drink to feast with after your ritual, preparing it all in advance will give you more time for contemplation after your ritual.

Preparing the Altar

The altar is the working space you create for your ritual, on which you will place all your tools and ingredients your ritual requires. The altar also acts as a focal point for the ceremony.

It can be a table, a box, a flat stone or piece of wood, in fact any flat raised structure will do. When deciding on the size keep in mind that all your working tools and symbols, as well as cakes & wine, will be kept on the altar for the duration of the ceremony.

All items on an altar are usually packed away after the ceremony, unless you are lucky enough to have a permanent ritual space which is dedicated as a temple. Packing away everything avoids unnecessary curiosity from friends and family and keeps things nice and tidy too! Remember, that an altar is a working table.

In Wicca, the altar is usually placed in the North, which is considered to be the place of mystery, although some traditions do place the altar in the East as it is the place of the rising Sun and of new beginnings. Solitaries can choose which they prefer, and might even want to alternate between North and East depending on the purpose of their ceremony. Another practice, which although rare, is used sometimes is that of putting the altar in the centre of the circle. This is practical if you are working in a large space, and is often used in larger group situations.

If you decide to do work with a particular element or something which likewise is attributed to a specific direction, you could place your altar in the corresponding part of the circle.

Some guidelines

You should place everything you will need for your ceremony on your altar and it is useful to make a checklist as part of your planning to ensure that nothing is forgotten.

The tools should generally be placed according to their elemental correspondences. So for instance, the pentacle should be placed on the northern side of the altar (element of Earth), the Chalice on the West (element of Water), the athame on the South side of the altar (element of Fire), the wand and censer on the East side of the altar (element of Air).

It is important to keep the altar practical, so you should place the tools you are likely to use more often during your ceremony, such as your wand or athame, near the front, keep them facing towards their respective elemental directions. All ingredients or other special tools for spells or other workings should also be placed in a convenient space, so that you will be able to reach them easily during your ceremony. It is, for instance, best to keep the salt and water bowls near the front of the altar, as this will make it easy to reach for the blessing and consecration.

The candles, one for the Goddess, one for the God and one for Spirit, should be placed near the back of the altar. The Goddess candle should be placed on the left and the God candle on the right. The positioning of the Goddess and God candles corresponds to the black and white pillars on the Qabalistic Tree of Life, representing the Goddess and God respectively. The Spirit candle should be in the centre. Having the candles towards the back of the altar helps prevent accidents when you are reaching for items on the altar, and also allows it to illuminate your altar more effectively. If you are using statues, pictures or symbolic representations of the Goddess and God, these should be placed in proximity to their respective candles.

Your altar should if possible be decorated with items that correspond to the purpose of your ritual. You may want to use altar cloths in appropriate colours to the planetary influences you are invoking, or which are sacred to the Goddess or God you are working with, or indeed the seasonal ritual you are performing. You can also use greenery or other images which are appropriate for your ritual. Altars can be as creative as you wish them to be, but do keep it practical! Using additional symbols, colours and images that correspond to the ritual you are performing will enhance your ritual, but too many may distract.

Preparing the Participants

By purifying ourselves we prepare ourselves for the practice of magick, and create a demarcation between the mundane and the magickal. The act of self-purification declares our intent to be in the best possible state to do magick and honour our Gods.

Ritual Baths

Before you start a ritual, having a purification bath will help you get into the right frame of mind. You may add appropriate essential oils, herbs or salts to your bath to enhance the process.

The purpose of the bath is purification, and it is the start of your ritual – so your mind should be focused purely on the matter at hand, you can combine the bath itself with visualisations and balancing work.

When you emerge from the bath, allow yourself to dry naturally. If it is not possible to have a ritual bath beforehand, at least try and wash your hands and face, especially for healing work!

Examples of oils & herbs that have purificatory properties include: frankincense, sandalwood, hyssop, St John's Wort and myrrh. You can also use sea salt.

Ritual baths can be combined with chanting or meditation relevant to the ritual you are about to perform.

Fasting

We can use fasting to cleanse our bodies from the inside. Fasting helps the body remove toxins and also means that all your energy will go into the ritual; rather than bodily functions such as digestion. A fast normally lasts a period of one day or longer, but it is important to remember that if you lead a busy life a fast of more than one day may be impractical.

When you fast, you should abstain from all food and stimulants. This means no caffeine, no alcohol and no tobacco! Not all Wiccans use fasting, and it is certainly not a prerequisite, although it can be a good way of strengthening your will.

Many people use fasting as a method of purification for important rituals, such as initiations – drinking only spring water and apple juice for a predetermined period, usually 24 hours.

Apples symbolise the Goddess and are considered the fruit of wisdom, and drinking apple juice ensures your blood sugar does not become too low or your energy become drained.

If you find that cutting out all food when fasting is a problem, try eating only certain types of food, like fruit. Some people find their metabolism struggles to cope with periods of fasting, and it is important that you use the form of fasting best for your body. If you have any health problems be sure to consult your doctor before attempting any period of fasting, especially if you plan on doing it for longer than 24 hours.

For most rituals it should not be necessary to fast for long periods of time, unless you are doing a specific ritual that requires it for some reason. It is still however a good idea to abstain from food and stimulants for at least 4 hours before a ritual, as this will aid any psychic work and will of course also make it easier for you to participate in dancing and movement without being slowed down by a heavy meal.

Anointing

Anointing can also effectively be used as part of pre-ritual purification. A special oil or ointment can be prepared containing herbs and oils which have purificatory properties, these can be blended with ingredients which are sacred to the Goddess or God who you will be working with, or they may have another special symbolic meaning related to your ceremony.

In groups, the participants should be anointed by the High Priestess or an appointed Priest or Priestess, accompanied with appropriate wording, such as *"Be pure of thought, Blessed Be!"* or *"Let wisdom enter herein".* The anointing is usually done on the third eye with a crescent Moon shape, or another suitable symbol. Any finger can be used for the anointing; we usually use the little finger of the dominant hand as was recorded to be the practice in ancient Egypt.

If you work as a solitary, you can still incorporate anointing as a part of your ritual preparation. Other applications for anointing include anointing the hands prior to healing and anointing the chakra energy centre points when performing balancing exercises.

Censing

Incense is a very effective tool for purification and can be used to cense (sometimes called smudging when done with bundles of herbs, rather than incense). Censing can be used in Wiccan ritual in a variety of ways for purification. Participants can be censed as they enter the circle, or prior to the circle being cast. The sacred space itself can be purified by censing the entire space prior to casting or after casting to purify and to welcome the Gods.

Scourging

In some Wiccan traditions scourging is used as a form of purification. This is not something you need to be concerned with as a solitary practitioner. However, if you dislike the idea, for whatever reason, then it is something you should ask about before joining a coven.

Grounding

No ritual can start or be completed without grounding. The term has a two-fold meaning:

Firstly we ground ourselves by centring our energy prior to a ritual. The best way of doing this is through the use of simple breathing and meditation techniques.

When a ritual is complete, we come to the second way in which grounding is used in Wiccan ritual – this time it is to ground the extra energy that we hold both within ourselves and the circle, to ensure that we are able to continue with our activities and that the ritual space is left in an appropriate energy state.

Most covens and working groups follow a ritual with a meal, which helps participants to reconnect with mundane reality and the physical world. The more earthing the food is, the better – carbohydrate rich dishes, such as rice, pasta, bread etc are all very good choices. You can also ground the energy by stamping your feet or touching your palms to the ground and letting the energy flow into the earth as you do so.

PART III – The Rituals

Purification of the ritual space

The ritual space is where you will cast your circle and perform your rituals, it is a place into which you will invite the Gods and it is considered sacred in Wicca for this reason. It is also important to carefully purify the space to ensure that no unwanted energies remain.

In Wiccan ritual this is done through the blessing of the salt and water on the altar and then sprinkling the space with the consecrated salt water. In Wicca salt is attributed to the element of Earth.

Water also has an important role in many religions for its cleansing properties, and it is easy to see why. Water washes away impurities and uncleanliness and can make something clean again. Water is also a key building block of life, without water there is no life.

Both the elements of Earth & Water are attributed to the feminine principle in Wicca, and on this level the symbolism of sprinkling a space with salt water can be seen as bringing in the qualities of the Goddess in preparation for the rite.

Symbolically water is associated with the Moon, with the realms of the astral planes and the tides of the unconscious. By mixing the water with the salt (earth), you are demonstrating that you will perform magic, bringing the subtle magickal energies (represented by water) through to manifestation in the physical world (represented by salt).

If you work in a group, it is usual for the High Priestess to perform the consecration of the water and the High Priest the salt. The High Priest will add the salt to the water and hand the bowl to the High Priestess, who will sprinkle the space herself, or hand the bowl to an appointed person in the Coven, in some traditions this will be the Coven maiden.

Another important point – when you sprinkle the circle, you should lustrate the entire space in which you will be working, not just the perimeter of the circle. Sprinkle the boundaries of the circle first, then sprinkle some of the water into the centre of the circle.

Water should be exorcised to render it pure and sacred, whereas the salt is usually only blessed, as it is considered to be pure already.

Some Wiccans have also included other techniques for purifying the space borrowed from other traditions. These include censing the space with incense or smudge sticks, shaking a rattle or beating a drum.

If you are working outdoors, it is worth keeping in mind that salt can be damaging to plant life, as such it might be more appropriate to use a purificatory herb, instead of salt when performing the purification of the space. Sage, St. John's Wort, Hyssop, Rosemary and Vervain are all good examples of herbs with purificatory properties.

The Consecration of Salt and Water

As you are performing the consecrations, you should place each bowl in turn on the pentacle, which is used as the base for consecrations.

Place the tip of your athame in the water, visualizing gold light directed from your heart along the energy channels in the arms, through the hands and directed down the blade of the athame into the water, saying:

> *I bless and consecrate this Water, that it be pure and untainted, in the names of the Goddess and the God. In love and truth, so mote it be!*

Do the same with the salt, directing energy in the same way through your athame into the salt, saying:

> *I bless and consecrate this Salt, symbol of purity and protection, in the names of the Goddess and the God. In love and truth, so mote it be!*

Now add some of the salt into the water, stirring the salt into the water in three clockwise circles, visualizing the salt water glowing with pure gold light.

Gold is the colour of the sun and success, a colour of purity, healing and achieving goals. By using gold in consecrations you are ensuring the purity of the item being consecrated and also that it will work to best effect.

If you are using a wand or your fingers, you will find it easier to tip a little of the salt into the water bowl rather than trying to use the end of the wand or your hands. You may also use the names of a specific Goddess or God, instead.

Once the salt water is consecrated, walk from your altar, around your space deosil from East to East, sprinkling the salt water as you go, saying:

Where this salt and water falls let all outside influences be gone. With salt and water I purify this space in love and truth. So mote it be!

Whilst you are doing this visualise the space being filled with a purifying golden light, the manifestation of the golden light you used to consecrate the salt and water being expressed into your ritual space.

The Magick Circle

In Wicca we create a magick circle in which we perform our rituals and devotions. The circle separates us from the mundane world so that we are transported to a "world between the worlds" ready to perform our magickal and devotional work. The magick circle is our working space for the duration of our rituals.

Once cast, it keeps us safe from that which we do not invite into the space as well as acting as a vessel to concentrate the energies we raise within it so that we may direct them with more ease towards our desired goals. It acts as a sacred space in which rituals may be performed.

In Wicca it is traditional to use the sword or athame to cast the circle, or in some instances the wand. When working in a coven, the casting is traditionally done by either the High Priestess or High Priest, according to the preferences of the coven or tradition. Of course if you are working solitary you do it yourself!

Movement within the circle should always be deosil, unless the movement is specifically intended to be symbolic of banishing, in which case it should be widdershins. This is rare and in some traditions this is considered bad luck, or negative. On occasion it can however be used to great effect in ritual, for banishing negativity or for seasonal rites in which (e.g.) Winter is banished and Spring is welcomed. Widdershins movement can also be used to open the circle, as a symbolic unwinding of the circle, to take us back from the magickal to the mundane world.

The magick circle has a great deal of symbolism in Wicca. As already mentioned, in Wicca we often talk of the magick circle as a place between the worlds, to indicate that we are transported to a domain that is nearer to our Gods when we perform our ceremonies.

The shape of the circle itself represents continuity and creation, fertility, equality and all celestial bodies and has a long tradition of use in history. It is also a symbol of unity, which is important on two levels: There is the unity of the coven working magick together, and the unity of the participants with the Gods.

The circle can be seen to represent the womb of the Earth Goddess, from which all creation sprang forth, and as such represents a place in which we can communicate with her. The shape of the circle may be seen as representing both the Moon and the Sun, as well as the eternal movement of the seasons through the wheel of the year.

The circle is also considered a symbol of perfection, as it has no beginning and no ending. Circles are very fluid shapes, with no corners to trap energy or act as points of manifestation. Think of the way a wheel rolls, and you appreciate the cyclic nature inherent in a circle.

Many groups do cast a circle to be the traditional nine foot in diameter, although more often the circle size is determined by the number of people participating, and in some instances the space available – if faced with a coven of thirteen or more members, a circle of only nine foot in diameter will not allow for much movement or dancing!

Casting a Circle

The traditional Wiccan method is to use the sword or athame to draw the circle. This is done because the sword and athame represent the will of the person wielding them, and are seen as a focus for the energy that is being directed. The wand can also be used, and is advised for rituals in which nature spirits are to be invoked as some, in particular the Faery, are known to dislike steel.

If you do not have an athame or wand you can cast and open the circle using your hand. This is normally done using the preferred hand with index and forefinger extended, ring and little fingers folded down, with the thumb folded over on top of them. You should feel a flow of energy from your body which accumulates in your hands

Walk deosil around the space, visualising the energy manifesting as blue flames at the tip of your athame (or sword, wand or fingers as appropriate), which marks the boundaries of your circle. A good way to visualise this is to see the flames shoot up and down to encapsulate you. Then as you move around the circle, see them spreading, increasing as you move around.

Blue is the colour of purity and psychism in the western Mystery Tradition, hence sapphire being the stone of purity and psychic awakening. Blue is also the colour associated with the heavens and the astral realms, thus its use in casting the circle, where you are moving beyond the physical realm to a place "between the worlds". It is interesting to note that the eminent psychologist and scientist Wilhelm Reich described the orgone energy as being blue in colour. This energy he saw as the sexual power inherent in us all.

As you walk the boundaries say:

> *I cast this circle, may this circle be a shield of protection and a boundary between the worlds. I bless thee and consecrate thee, in the names of the Goddess and God. The Circle is Cast. So mote it be!*

A version we sometimes use is one we created which includes the elements in the casting itself. As you walk around casting the circle, say:

By fertile Earth and whirling Air,
By rushing Fire and Water fair,
By Spirit joined and all held fast,
This sacred circle now is cast!

Once you are comfortable with the standard circle casting, you can try other methods if they appeal to you and see how they feel. E.g. some people like to walk the boundary of the circle beating a drum or ringing a bell, or carrying incense (such as a censer, joss stick or smudge bundle).

Circles are cast deosil (sunwise), starting and finishing in the East (the place of the Sunrise).

Guardians of the Four Elements

Once the circle has been cast, the next step in a Wiccan ceremony is the invocation of the Watchtowers – also known as the calling of the Guardians of the Four Elements. This is another idea we find in ancient Egypt, where guardian deities were often called to protect the space at the four quarters.

When invoking the guardians of the Watchtowers, we are calling upon the elemental energies of Air, Fire, Water and Earth to join us in our circle. The four elements combined bring balance and create the fifth element of Spirit. In Wiccan ritual we call upon a guardian from each of the elements to both help protect our circle at each cardinal point and to bless the circle (and those within) with their energies and qualities.

As you call the element raise your arms in the blessing position. This is done by raising your arms so they form a "V", with your palms open and facing forwards. As you say *"I bid you hail and welcome"*, cross your arms making an "X" across your chest and give a little bow. This is a mark of respect as you welcome the guardian of the element. The same gestures are used when you bid them farewell.

The elements are called starting in the East, place of Air and new beginnings. You then turn deosil to the South to call Fire, then to the West to call Water and to the North to call Earth, finally turning back to the East to complete the circular motion.

In our group we prefer to invite the elements rather than commanding them. The traditional manner of "summoning, stirring and calling up" implies dominance over the elements, rather than a harmony with them. We do not feel this is appropriate to Wiccan ritual as it emphasises "power over" rather than "power with". What is important, especially if you work in a group, is to keep a uniformity throughout. This might seem formulaic at first, but prevents one person from doing a 5 second invocation followed by the next person doing a 15 minute speech – if this happens it will hinder the flow of the ritual rather than aid it regardless of how good the invocations are! Also having a set way of calling quarters in a group helps build confidence as everyone will be able to learn the words beforehand!

Invoking the Guardians of the Elements

The following is an example of how the elements are invited into the circle. You can adapt the words to suit a particular ritual or to your own personal preference, maybe including some of the correspondences of each of the elements.

Example:

> (Facing East)
> *Powers of Air, I call to you now and invite you to join me in this rite, to share your qualities with me; In Love and Truth, I bid you Hail and Welcome!*
>
> (Facing South)
> *Powers of Fire, I call to you now and invite you to join me in this rite, to share your qualities with me; In Love and Truth, I bid you Hail and Welcome!*
>
> (Facing West)
> *Powers of Water, I call to you now and invite you to join me in this rite, to share your qualities with me; In Love and Truth, I bid you Hail and Welcome!*
>
> (Facing North)
> *Powers of Earth, I call to you now and invite you to join me in this rite, to share your qualities with me; In Love and Truth, I bid you Hail and Welcome!*

If this is done in a group, you would say *"we"* rather than *"I"* and *"us"* rather than *"me"* when performing the calling and the farewells.

The Guardians of the Elements are commonly referred to as the Lords and Ladies of the Watchtowers. Within this context the Guardians of Air and Fire (the masculine elements) are usually seen as masculine (Lords) and the Guardians of Water and Earth (the feminine elements) as feminine (Ladies).

The Air Guardian is a very tall, slender and beautiful man with very ethereal features, piercing grey eyes and blonde hair. He is dressed in gossamer thin yellow robes that blow around his body, and has a crown of white lilies on his head. He may be visualised standing on a wind-swept hill or in the elemental landscape of air.

The Fire Guardian is tall and powerfully built with strong musculature. He has sharp features and red hair and flaming red-brown eyes. He is dressed in scarlet robes, and has a crown of red poppies on his head. He may be visualised standing on a volcano or in the elemental landscape of fire.

The Water Guardian is a voluptuous and very beautiful woman with grey-green hair and deep blue eyes. She is dressed in flowing blue robes, and has a crown of blue lotuses on her head. She may be visualised standing in front of a waterfall or on the seashore, or in the elemental landscape of water.

The Earth Guardian is a well built and very beautiful woman with dark brown hair and green eyes. She is dressed in green robes, and has a crown of corn on her head. She may be visualised standing in a corn field in front of woods, or in the elemental landscape of earth.

The elementals of all the elements, both male and female, may also be seen in these descriptions when they are visualised in human form.

Some groups call the Archangels of the Elements as worked with in ritual magick in the Pentagram ritual. These are Raphael (Air), Michael (Fire), Gabriel (Water) and Uriel (Earth). All of the archangels are seen with large white wings on their backs. If you wish to work with the archangels they are visualised as follows:

Raphael stands around 9ft tall, his face almost too bright to see, very beautiful and androgynous. He wears a yellow robe, and there are flashes of purple about his form, he holds a caduceus and the air element enters the circle from behind him in the East. You may feel a flow of air like gentle breezes blowing past Raphael into the circle.

Michael also stands around 9ft tall, with a beautiful radiant masculine face. His robe is bright red and there are flashes of green around him as he holds a sword or lance in his right hand. Flames dance around Michael's feet, and from the South you feel the heat as the element of fire enters the circle.

Gabriel stands around 9ft tall, his face blindingly bright, beautiful and feminine. He wears a blue robe and holds aloft a silver chalice, around his form there are flashes of orange. You may also see a waterfall behind Gabriel, and from behind him in the West you feel cool moisture as the element of water enters the circle.

Uriel stands around 9ft tall, his face beautiful and feminine, with a look of nurturing and compassion on it. His robe is of green, with flashes of red about him. He holds a pentacle and stands in front of a field of corn with woods behind. You sense the impending strength and stability of earth, and from the North behind him you feel the element of Earth enter the circle.

Invoking the Goddess & God

There are two ways in which this is usually done in a Wiccan ceremony. The first is an invocation of the Goddess and God into the circle, and the second, which is commonly used by covens, is Drawing Down the Moon (Goddess) and Drawing Down the Sun (God) in which the deities are invoked into a Priestess or Priest.

Drawing Down the Moon and Drawing down the Sun as practiced in Wicca require at least two people. This is usually a Priest who invokes the Goddess into a Priestess, who then acts as a channel for the Goddess. She in turn then invokes the God into the Priest, who acts as a vessel for the God. When the Priestess or Priest enters a trance state during this ceremony they channel both the energy and the words of the Goddess or God, and in some instances may not remember much of the experience, or what they said afterwards. This is another reason why this is usually not done by solitaries in the same way.

In some covens and traditions the Priestess and Priest only enter a partial trance, during which they recite a prepared "charge". This charge usually takes the form of a piece of prose prepared in advance, the best known example being the well known *"Charge of the Goddess"*. In our own covens, Priestesses and Priests use both prepared charges and full trance states when performing this part of the ritual, depending on what is most appropriate.

Invocation of the Goddess also brings the energy of the Goddess into the circle, but in a different way. When you invoke a Goddess you are asking her to bring her blessings and energy into your circle. This technique is used by both solitaries and covens alike, and can be a very powerful way in which to explore the mysteries of different deities.

Drawing down can be seen as the person who is drawn down on being the gateway for the energy of the Goddess or God, whereas invocation is making the whole circle the gateway for the energy of the Goddess or God.

Books and other sources can provide many examples of invocations which you can use. It is of course better to write your own, but first using examples from other people, and older examples such as the Orphic Hymns, can provide a great source of inspiration.

Example:
(adaptation from the Orphic Hymns, Hymn to Hekate)

> *I invoke thee beloved Lady of magick*
> *Hekate of the Crossroads*
> *Hekate of the three-ways*
> *Of the Heavens, Earth & Sea*
> *Saffron-cloaked Goddess of the Heavens*
> *Nightgoing one, Protectress of dogs*
> *Unconquerable Queen*
> *I ask you to be present now at this my sacred rite*
> *To bless me and protect me!*

Spend some time researching the Goddess or God you are looking to invoke, research their mythologies, their symbols and their roles within the pantheon in which they originate. Including symbolism and titles of a deity in your invocations can be a great way of making it a more powerful and personal experience. Of course through knowing more about the deities you work with, it also becomes easier for you to foster a closer relationship with them.

When you invoke a Goddess or God you should visualise that deity in the way they have usually been portrayed in the art of their culture. E.g. Artemis was depicted as a tall and beautiful maiden in a white hunting tunic carrying a bow with her quiver of arrows on her back. See the deity coming to your circle from their realm and standing over your circle, so their presence fills the space. So e.g. for chthonian deities you may see the deity rising from the ground, for stellar, solar and lunar deities they may descend from the sky, etc.

It is preferable to memorise the invocation if you can, as you can focus more on the energy of the deity and visualizing them if you are not reading from a piece of paper. With practice you will find you can do invocations spontaneously without needing to prepare, especially if it is deities that you have worked with a lot and are familiar with.

Invocation of the Goddess

Example:

> *Beautiful and graceful Lady of the Moon*
> *Goddess of the tides of life*
> *Lady of Magick and Mystery*
> *You who are the giver and taker of life*
> *I ask you to join me now in this rite*
> *To inspire me and to guide me on my path*
> *Bountiful and wise Goddess of the Night*
> *Join me now, as I do bid thee hail and welcome*

Invocation of the God

Example:

> *Mighty Horned God of the Woodlands*
> *Bringer of magick and mystery,*
> *God of Life, Light and Liberty*
> *Who guard the wild and free places*
> *I ask you to join me now in this rite*
> *To share your wild wisdom with me*
> *Strong and gentle guardian of the wild animals,*
> *Join me now, as I do bid thee hail and welcome!*

Ritual Content

Of course a ritual is not just about creating a magickal space and invoking the Gods, although both these play an important part. The purpose of your ceremony will determine what else you do during the ritual.

The following are some examples of what you may include, every ceremony is unique however, so you may include a mixture of these or just one, you may even have other ideas to add!

Whether quiet and contemplative or loud and raucous, celebration is a key element of Wicca. It sums up the difference between Wicca and a number of other religions.

Of course all Wiccan rituals are devotions to the Gods. We celebrate our Gods, rather than prostrating ourselves, and the phrase *"all acts of love and pleasure are my rituals"* from the Charge of the Goddess encapsulates the way in which we work with our Gods. We also never denigrate our Gods by placing the responsibility of our actions onto them, as we take personal responsibility for our actions.

You may want to however include a specific devotional component to your ritual at certain times. It can be an interesting and effective way in which to develop your understanding and relationship with the Gods that you work with, and the form that such a ritual devotion will take will largely depend on your relationship and understanding of the Gods.

There are also of course specific practices associated with some of the Goddesses and Gods, and you may want to include something historic in your ritual. For example, making cakes with ingredients sacred to the Greek Goddess Hekate (such as saffron & onion) and leaving them at crossroads on the dark moon, or lighting candles for the Irish Goddess Bride at Imbolc (Candlemas).

You can also prepare incense with ingredients sacred to the Goddess or God you are working with and burn that whilst reciting some inspirational poetry, chanting or singing. Of course you could keep it very simple and simply light a candle in their honour and spend some time in quiet contemplation and communion.

If you are performing a ceremony in celebration of the turning of the Wheel of the Year, you may want to include celebrations and workings which are specific to that time of the year.

Examples:

Beltane – Gather dew first thing in the morning and use it in spells for beauty and youthfulness. If you are working in a group you can erect a maypole and include that in your ceremony. Solitaries can tie wish ribbons to trees.

Litha – Rise to greet the Sun on the morning of Midsummer and perform a ceremony to honour the Solar Gods.

Lughnasadh - making a corn dolly with some of the harvest grain to symbolise fertility for your projects in the coming year. If you have a corn dolly you made in a previous year you could offer it to the Goddess and return it to the Earth.

Samhain – If you are working in a group, apple bobbing can be great fun (albeit messy!). Samhain is also a traditional time to perform divination and skrying is particularly appropriate.

By performing devotional and celebrational work, you develop a stronger bond with the Gods, and this is important, because Wicca does not act through intermediaries, the emphasis is on your own personal relationship with the Gods of Wicca.

Remember that the Gods like to have fun too, and can have a wicked sense of humour!

Spells

This is the part of the ritual where you perform spells, i.e. magickal workings towards a specified goal, such as a job spell, wealth spell, healing spell, etc. Remember spells do not have to be hurried, and you will find that a reasonable amount of time spent in raising energy, and focusing your intent and the visualisation of your goal will greatly increase the effectiveness of your workings.

Our experience has been that it is better to do fewer spells in a ceremony, and do more than one ceremony, rather than to perform dozens of spells in a single ceremony. Not only will your altar be cluttered with spell ingredients, but you will also be flagging when it comes to raising energy and clearly focusing your intent after a few spells.

Ideally you should not do more than about two or three spells in a ritual, any more than that and you will probably start losing concentration. This is as true for solitaries as it is for covens, as raising energy, holding visualisations and preparing for each spell in turn, takes a great deal of energy and time.

Many people enjoy casting spells, and many do not, seeing them as not being spiritual. Spells are performed for a purpose, and that purpose is to create positive change. To this end it is beneficial to not be too zealous about never performing spells, but rather to perform them when you need them. If everything in your life is going wonderfully, you may not wish to cast spells; conversely e.g. if a close friend or relative is ill, you may perform a lot of healing spells (with their permission) to help them recover.

Spell techniques which may be used in a Wiccan ritual include:

★ Candle Spells

The use of candles to perform spells is widely used today and can be an effective, yet simple way of performing spells. The basic technique involves choosing a candle of an appropriate colour, carving it with symbols which represent the desired outcome, anointing it with oils which correspond to the desired outcome and then ritually charging it, by using chanting, singing, dancing or concentration. Finally the candle is burned down to release the energy towards the desired outcome.

* Cord Magick

There are many examples of knot magick throughout history, well known examples can be found in ancient Greece and Egypt, as well as during more recent times, when it was used by Cunning folk in Devon and Cornwall to tie winds into knots, which were sold to sailors. The sailors would release the knots when they needed wind in their sails!

* Charms

Charms have long been used in magickal systems the world over to help protect from (amulet) or attract (talisman) a specific energy to the bearer. They can be simple in construction such as a magickally charged crystal; or complex such as a charm bag with a number of different ingredients and symbols which are used for their combined powers (charm bags are also magickally charged).

Of course there are many more ways of performing spells, it is a huge subject and many books have been published on the subject in recent years.

Dancing

Dancing whilst chanting is one of the most commonly used, effective and simple ways to raise energy for spells and celebration. In groups dancing is usually performed deosil in a circle, or in a spiral.

Whilst the dancing is done people also visualise the energy generated by their movement and singing as a particular colour, such as gold or blue, forming an inverted cone of energy within the circle. By combining the energy of the dance, the singing and the visualisation, a lot of energy can be generated to power spells or other magickal work. The High Priestess or person leading the ritual will allow the dancing to go on until she feels enough energy has been raised to be directed by her to the desired intent.

Singing and Chanting

If you are working solitary or have space constraints on your group, you may prefer to chant without dancing. In such instances you are concentrating on the sound produced by your voice as the primary form of generated energy. The energy you raise through singing chants for a period of time is again visualised as a swirling pattern of appropriately coloured energy which you allow to build up until you feel there is enough to power your intent for the spell or whatever the purpose is.

Divination

There may be times that you find you need help with big questions or dilemmas that you face in your every day life. Instead of doing a spell for this, you could perform a divination as part of your ritual. Of course most forms of divination can be practiced outside a magick circle, but you may want to perform it in a circle to ensure additional energy and blessings from the Gods or for a purpose related to previous spell work like healing to see how the magick is working.

Forms of divination which you may want to explore for use within a Wiccan ritual include:

Tarot

The use of Tarot cards, and oracle cards can bring an interesting dimension to Wiccan ritual. There are so many different decks of cards available today which you can choose from depending on the nature and theme of your ritual. We often use the *Thoth Tarot* (by Lady Frieda Harris & Aleister Crowley) for yearly divinations, or the *Druid Animal Oracle* (by Phillip & Stephanie Carr-Gomm) when we are working with Celtic deities, which are also excellent for power animal work. It is worth looking at and exploring the symbolism of different decks and finding those which resonate best with your interests and way of working.

Skrying

Skrying into a crystal ball has long been one of the archetypal images of witches, however there are many other methods of skrying which may suit you or your ritual. Fire skrying using a candle flame or a bowl with white spirit in to see patterns in the flame (be careful with flammable liquids!) is a technique that many witches find works well for them. Alternatively skrying in a magick mirror, or incense smoke, or candle wax dripped into a bowl of water are all other examples of ways you can use different mediums to skry in.

Ritual Drama

Ritual drama can be a very powerful technique in group work. Ritual drama is often included in celebrational rituals and sometimes in initiations. Participants take the roles of deities and/or heroes to illustrate and explore themes from particular myths. By taking the role of a particular deity or figure insights into the nature of the character or yourself can also be gained.

Consecration of the Cakes & Wine

The ceremony of the Blessing of the Cakes & Wine takes place after most of the work and celebration are done in the circle. Some groups use the time after the blessing of cakes & wine to discuss experiences during the ceremony, feast in the circle after the ceremony or use the time to make announcements – others will close the circle after the partaking of cakes & wine and discuss the ceremony afterwards whilst feasting.

If you work solitary it is best to close the circle after the blessing of cakes & wine and then ground through feasting.

Blessing the Wine

The blessing of the wine in Wicca represents the sacred marriage as it symbolises the union of Goddess & God, considered to be one of the key mysteries of Wicca, which can only be fully understood through direct experience.

The Chalice symbolises the womb of the Fruitful Goddess, the wine shows the fecundity of the Earth and symbolises the joy in this life. It is traditional to use red wine, but mead or if you prefer apple or grape juice, can also be used. The athame represents the phallus of the Horned God, the fertilizing principle.

Symbolically the chalice and athame represent the elements of water and fire, and when the triangular symbols of these two elements are conjoined, they produce the hexagram, representing the universe. The sacred marriage of the two divine principles is thus expressed in the creation of the universe through their union, embodied in the sacramental drink within the chalice as their life-giving fertility.

The fruit juices used have specific symbolisms. Apple juice represents the fruit of wisdom, sacred to the Goddess and containing the pentagram within it. Grape juice is the fruit of the vine, sacred to the God as the Lord of Liberation and Wildness, in forms such as the Greek Dionysus and Roman Bacchus.

When working in a group it is usual for the High Priestess and High Priest to perform the ceremony together. The High Priest holds the Chalice, and the High Priestess lowers the athame into the Chalice saying:

> *As the Athame is to the Male so the Cup is to the Female and conjoined they bring forth fruitfulness.*

The High Priestess drinks from the Chalice first, then passes the Chalice to the High Priest with a kiss and the words *"Blessed Be"* or *"May you never thirst"*. The High Priest then passes the Chalice to the person next to him in the circle with the same words and the Chalice is passed from person to person, each time with a kiss and *"Blessed Be"* or *"May you never thirst"*.

It is traditional that the High Priestess is given the remaining wine in the cup to finish, or when working outdoors she will take a last sip and then make a libation with the remaining wine to the Old Ones.

For solitary work you should hold the athame in your dominant hand, and the chalice in your other hand. As you do so imagine the energy of the God descending down the blade of the athame into the wine, like a flash of golden lightning, and the energy of the Goddess permeating the wine, like a flowing silver tide, from the chalice that symbolises her womb (the same visualisations are used for group work as described above).

Example:

Take the Chalice and hold it up saying:

> *I bless this wine, made from the fruits of this bountiful Earth, fertile and nurturing, blessed by the union of the Goddess and God. Blessed be.*

Then take a sip of the wine and replace the Chalice on the altar.

Blessing the Cakes

The cakes form part of the grounding of the ritual and also symbolise the fruitfulness of the Goddess and God, as well as symbolising the gifts given to us by the Earth herself.

The cakes traditionally should be made with flour, wine, a pinch of salt and honey, which are then shaped into crescent moons. In practice most groups working together will use cakes, bread or biscuits which reflect the celebration. For instance it is perfectly acceptable to use a *Yule Log* when celebrating Yule, bread baked from corn for Lughnasadh, or something sweet for Beltane!

When working in a group it is traditional to have one more cake than the number of celebrants for the blessing. The cakes are blessed by the High Priestess, who touches each cake with the tip of her athame, visualizing the golden energy flowing from her through the athame into the cakes.

She takes the first cake and breaks it into two pieces, giving half to the High Priest with a kiss and say *"Blessed be"* or *"May you never hunger"*. He then passes the pentacle with the cakes to the celebrant next to him with a kiss and *"Blessed Be"* or *"May you never hunger"* and so it is passed from one person to the next until it is returned to the altar. The High Priestess will take the remaining cakes and make a libation to the Old Ones.

An alternative to the athame is for the High Priestess to use the wand for the blessing of the cakes. This then means all four of the elemental tools have been used in the Cakes & Wine – chalice and athame for wine, and pentacle and wand for cakes.

When working solitary, hold your hands over the pentacle and visualise golden energy flowing through your hands down into the cakes as you say:

> *I bless these cakes, made from the seeds of the grain grown in the bosom of the earth, fertile and bountiful, blessed by the grace of the Goddess and the vitality and strength of the God.*

Break the cake in half and eat half – replacing the remaining part on the pentacle or libate it if you are working outdoors. Alternatively you can touch your athame or wand to the cakes and see the golden energy flow from your hands through the tool into the cakes rather than use your hands when you bless the cakes.

Farewell to the God & Goddess

At the end of your ceremony you say farewell to the God first, as the end of the ritual is in reverse order to the beginning. This can be very simple, and should thank him, acknowledging his power and properties. An example of this would be as given below for Cernunnos.

Example:

> Mighty Cernunnos, Lord of the Wild Beasts and the Wild Places, Guardian of the Old Ways, I thank you for joining me and sharing your power and timeless wisdom with me, In love and joy and truth, I bid you hail and farewell.

As you say the "Hail and Farewell" you should bow in honour of his presence, power and courtesy. See him walking, flying or descending away back to his realm, in a similar manner to how you saw him arrive.

The farewell to the Goddess follows exactly the same formula as the farewell to the God. If you are working solitary you will do both of these farewells. In a group, the person who invoked a God or Goddess is always the one who also bids farewell.

Example:

> Beautiful Goddess, I thank you for joining me and bestowing your gifts on me,
> You will always dwell in my heart and my spirit,
> But for now as I end this rite
> I bid you hail and farewell.

Banishing the Guardians

Obviously when you have finished your rite you say farewell to the Elemental Guardians, starting in the North with Earth and moving widdershins to Air in the East.

This is done before opening the circle, as the closing of a rite is done in reverse as a symbolic unwinding of the circle. As you speak see the Elemental Guardian leaving and returning to their realm, taking the elemental energy with them that they brought into the circle.

Example:

> (Facing North)
> *Powers of Earth, I thank you for joining me and sharing your qualities with me in this rite, and with love and joy and thanks I bid you Hail and Farewell.*

> (Facing West)
> *Powers of Water, I thank you for joining me and sharing your qualities with me in this rite, and with love and joy and thanks I bid you Hail and Farewell.*

> (Facing South)
> *Powers of Fire, I thank you for joining me and sharing your qualities with me in this rite, and with love and joy and thanks I bid you Hail and Farewell.*

> (Facing East)
> *Powers of Air, I thank you for joining me and sharing your qualities with me in this rite, and with love and joy and thanks I bid you Hail and Farewell.*

Whatever gestures you used to call the Elements should also be used in banishing. So if you made the elemental gestures, do so again, if you used invoking elemental pentagrams, use banishing elemental pentagrams, etc.

As you do this, feel the energy of the element leaving the circle. If you did use pentagrams visualise the elemental energy leaving through the pentagon in the centre of the pentagram, returning to its elemental landscape.

The pentagram that has been in the air at each quarter as a gateway for the elemental force should be seen disappearing as you draw the banishing pentagrams if you have used elemental pentagrams.

Opening the Circle

At the end of a ritual, the circle is opened by reversing the casting. This is done by again walking the boundaries of the circle, using your athame / wand or hand in the same way that you did for the casting of the circle.   This time you walk in the opposite direction to the way you walked when you cast the circle.

Whilst you walk you visualise the blue flames dying away and you say:
> *The rite is ended, the boundary removed as I return to the world of men, the circle is open yet unbroken!*

Record your experiences

As soon as you have finished your ceremony, you should write up your experience while it is still fresh in your mind. You will already have the structure recorded from when you planned the ritual, but now you should record details of your impressions of each part of the ritual and how it went. Any images, thoughts, words or impressions that you received at any time during the ritual should be recorded, and also how well or not you felt the different parts of the ritual went.

Be honest with yourself when recording the ritual. Rituals do not always go 100% according to plan, and things do not always work as you expect them to. By keeping honest and meticulous records, you can look back later and assess the effectiveness of different techniques of energy raising and spell casting, and see what works best for you.

Likewise when you record you may find it helpful to note factors such as the weather, your mood, and if you are a woman, the phase of your own menstrual cycle. Looking at such factors over time may give you indicators of times when you work particularly well or badly that you can figure in to your ceremonies.

PART IV – Ritual Refinements

Planetary Considerations

For spells the timing of your ritual can be critical. If you are using planetary energies in your spell, then you should take into account the day of the week and the time of day. Each day of the week corresponds to one of the seven classical planets, and if possible your spell should be done on the appropriate day for the nature of the spell.

Thus you would perform spells that are Saturnian on Saturday, Solar on Sunday, Lunar on Monday, Martial on Tuesday, Mercurial on Wednesday, Jupiterian on Thursday, and Venusian on Friday. Additionally you can further reinforce the focus of planetary energy in your spell by performing it during the appropriate planetary hour. Planetary hours originate in the medieval Grimoires, and are a simple system of working out the best time of day or night to work with the planetary energy you desire.

Calculating Planetary Hours

The planetary hours are not the same as the sixty-minute hours beginning at midnight that we use for normal timekeeping. The planetary days are divided into twenty-four planetary hours starting with the first hour of the day beginning at Sunrise, and ending with the last hour of the day ending at Sunrise of the next planetary day.

The period of daylight that extends from Sunrise to Sunset is divided into the twelve "hours" of the day. The period of darkness extending from Sunset to Sunrise of the next day is divided into the twelve "hours" of night. Combined these give the twenty-four hours of the planetary day.

As the duration of daylight and darkness varies except at the Spring and Autumn Equinoxes, on a particular planetary day the length of the hours of the day will differ from the length of the hours of the night. This is why the planetary hours are sometimes called the unequal hours. Almanacs and ephemeredes are sources to discover the Sunrise and Sunset times to enable you to calculate the planetary hours.

Attributions For The Hours Of The Day

Hour	Sunday	Monday	Tuesday	Wednesday	Thursday	Friday	Saturday
1	Sun	Moon	Mars	Mercury	Jupiter	Venus	Saturn
2	Venus	Saturn	Sun	Moon	Mars	Mercury	Jupiter
3	Mercury	Jupiter	Venus	Saturn	Sun	Moon	Mars
4	Moon	Mars	Mercury	Jupiter	Venus	Saturn	Sun
5	Saturn	Sun	Moon	Mars	Mercury	Jupiter	Venus
6	Jupiter	Venus	Saturn	Sun	Moon	Mars	Mercury
7	Mars	Mercury	Jupiter	Venus	Saturn	Sun	Moon
8	Sun	Moon	Mars	Mercury	Jupiter	Venus	Saturn
9	Venus	Saturn	Sun	Moon	Mars	Mercury	Jupiter
10	Mercury	Jupiter	Venus	Saturn	Sun	Moon	Mars
11	Moon	Mars	Mercury	Jupiter	Venus	Saturn	Sun
12	Saturn	Sun	Moon	Mars	Mercury	Jupiter	Venus

Attributions For The Hours Of The Night

Hour	Sunday	Monday	Tuesday	Wednesday	Thursday	Friday	Saturday
1	Jupiter	Venus	Saturn	Sun	Moon	Mars	Mercury
2	Mars	Mercury	Jupiter	Venus	Saturn	Sun	Moon
3	Sun	Moon	Mars	Mercury	Jupiter	Venus	Saturn
4	Venus	Saturn	Sun	Moon	Mars	Mercury	Jupiter
5	Mercury	Jupiter	Venus	Saturn	Sun	Moon	Mars
6	Moon	Mars	Mercury	Jupiter	Venus	Saturn	Sun
7	Saturn	Sun	Moon	Mars	Mercury	Jupiter	Venus
8	Jupiter	Venus	Saturn	Sun	Moon	Mars	Mercury
9	Mars	Mercury	Jupiter	Venus	Saturn	Sun	Moon
10	Sun	Moon	Mars	Mercury	Jupiter	Venus	Saturn
11	Venus	Saturn	Sun	Moon	Mars	Mercury	Jupiter
12	Mercury	Jupiter	Venus	Saturn	Sun	Moon	Mars

Example:

Let us say you wanted to work out the planetary hours for a spell that used Mercurial energies, e.g. to pass an exam. Wednesday is the day of Mercury, so you decide to perform the spell on the first Wednesday following the new Moon. The process is then as follows:

Consulting an almanac you see the Sun rises at 7am on that day and sets at 8.36pm. So the hours of daylight are from 07.00 – 20:36, giving 13 hours and 36 minutes.

13 x 60 + 36 = 816 minutes of daylight on that day. Divided by 12 = 68. So each of the 12 "hours" of daylight will be 68 minutes long.

Consulting the tables given you see the first and eighth hours of Wednesday are ruled by Mercury. So for the first hour of the day the spell should be performed between 7.00am and 8.08am (68 minutes).

For the eighth hour more calculation is involved. Add together the "hour" length for 7 "hours" (7 x 68 = 476 minutes, or 7 hours and 56 minutes). Then add this to the Sunrise time (7:00am) + 7 hours and 56 minutes = 2:56pm). This means the eighth hour starts at 2:56pm and finishes at 4:04pm (2:56 + 68 minutes).

You then decide which of these two times will be more practical, and you have your time to perform the spell in.

If you had instead decided to perform your spell in the hours of night, you can work out how long the night hours are by subtracting the length of the daylight "hour" from 120 minutes (2 hours), so in this instance the night "hours" would be 52 minutes long each (120 – 68). The first night hour starts at Sunset, so in this instance from 8.36pm to 9.28pm (52 minutes later).

Planetary Aspects

If you want to go even further with planetary energies, you can also look at the planetary aspects for the day you are planning on working your magick on. Planetary aspects can be found in some magazines (especially astrological ones). Positive or reinforcing aspects are conjunctions, trines and sextiles. Negative or challenging aspects are oppositions and squares.

Lunar Timing

The use of phases of the Moon is a major consideration in Wicca. The New Moon is the time for performing magick for beginning new projects. The Waxing Moon is the time for things you want to grow and increase, or attract to you. The Full Moon is a time of fruition and completion.

The Waning Moon is a time for getting rid of things you want to lose, which also includes healing when you are getting rid of illness. The Dark Moon is a time of transformation, of moving between phases.

To this we may also add the significant time of the Half Moon – when the face of the Moon shows equal light and dark. This is a very good time for balancing work. You can do work that needs to balance lighter qualities on the waxing Half Moon, and work that concentrates on balancing darker qualities (this includes the unconscious) on the waning Half Moon.

You may also wish to consider the symbolism of the Lunar Month for your spell work. The symbols associated with each lunar month can be incorporated into spell work, or even used as the theme for Esbats.

To the Celts trees were very sacred, and the Celtic Lunar Calendar ascribes a tree to each lunar month. There were regional variations as to which tree fitted which month, and they vary annually. As a rough guide, the calendar starts with Birch at the first New Moon after Yule and runs through the thirteen trees of the table below.

Tree	Key Words
Birch	Cleansing, new beginnings
Rowan	Protection against magick, control of the senses
Alder	Prophecy, spiritual protection
Willow	Feminine, lunar rhythms, fertility
Ash	Passage between inner and outer worlds

Hawthorn	Cleansing, chastity, protection, restraint
Oak	Solid protection, doorway to the mysteries, strength
Holly	Victory, fatherhood, vigour
Hazel	Intuition, wisdom, poetry, divination, inspiration
Apple	Beauty, wisdom, choice, immortality
Vine	Prophecy, letting go of inhibitions, instinct, emotions
Ivy	Spiral of the self and inner journey, transformation
Reed	Direct action, searching out basic truths

An occasion which happens about once every two and a half years you may wish to take advantage of is the Blue Moon. The Blue Moon occurs when there are two full Moons in a month, and is the second full Moon in a month. On rare occasions, such as in 1999, this can happen more than once a year. Obviously as they are 28 days apart this means the first full Moon needs to happen in the first day or two of the month.

The expression "once in a blue Moon" comes from this term, referring to an unusual event. Blue Moons are considered very magickal, and are a good time to work for things that are difficult to achieve – they can be seen as a window of opportunity to do that spell or ritual that really needs to work and work well.

Of course on these occasions the Moon does not actually turn blue, there are however occasions when it does! An example of this would be when the Indonesian volcano Krakatoa exploded in 1883, it sending dust clouds into the atmosphere which caused the Moon to appear blue all around the world for the best part of two years. (It also turned sunsets green!) The same phenomena can take place when large forest fires send smoke and dust particles into the air, although most of these instances are localised. Ice particles and clouds can also sometimes cause this to happen.

Solar Timing

The movement of the Sun through the heavens is reflected both in our daily and our annual lives. The Sun rises from dawn (Sunrise) to the midpoint of the day (from the point of view of the duration between Sunrise and Sunset) when the Sun is at its zenith, and this is the time for solar work seeking to increase qualities associated with the Sun. Likewise from the midpoint to Sunset would be a time for getting rid of negative solar qualities, or working to transform them into positive ones.

The Sabbats in the light half of the year from Spring Equinox to Autumn Equinox (when there is more light than dark in the day) could be performed during daylight hours, especially if a solar deity is being invoked.

Many megalithic monuments were built with alignment towards the Sun on the morning of the Summer and Winter solstices, and indeed sunrise on the morning of the Summer solstice makes an ideal time to celebrate the power of the Sun which is at its zenith. At the Midwinter solstice, we welcome the reborn Sun as the child of promise at dawn.

Although Wicca is often thought of as a lunar religion performed at night, remember that it is also about balance, so take advantage of the solar phases where they are appropriate!

The Cycles of Nature

In Wicca we attune to the cyclic nature of the Earth through the celebration of her seasons. The festivals, which are also called Sabbats, are celebrated at eight turning points throughout the year. This cycle of eight festivals is known to Wiccans as the Wheel of the Year.

The Wiccan Sabbats – Samhain (Halloween), Yule (Midwinter), Imbolc (Candlemas, Bride), Eostra (Spring Equinox, Ostara), Beltane (May day), Litha (Midsummer), Lughnasadh (Lammas) and Modron (Autumn Equinox, Mabon) – help us to tune in with the cycles of nature as they exist both within us and in the world around us.

Although we know almost for certain that the combination of the eight festivals into what is known as the "Wheel of the Year" today, is a modern concept, and that no one group of people would have celebrated all eight of the festivals in the same way as we do today, there is absolutely no doubt that all the festivals marking the points on the wheel are rooted in history.

The Wheel of the Year is so called for a good reason – wheels turn and return to the same point, but never quite the same place, and the wheel of Nature continues to turn, each season containing many new wonders.

Observation and celebration of these seasons will help you to become more attuned to the energies of Nature each year, it is a process that never stops. No one person can ever be an expert on the nature of Nature!

There is no one correct way of celebrating any of these festivals, and within the context of this book they are included here for the sake of completion.

The following are key themes which may provide inspiration when you are preparing for your own celebrations:

Festival	Date	Key Themes
Samhain	31st October	Ancestors, Beginnings, Divination, Harvest (Meat), Facing Shadow, Transformation
Yule	21st December	Rebirth of the Sun, Resolutions, Turning Tide
Imbolc	1st February	First Stirrings, Initiation, Psychic Abilities
Eostra	21st March	Balance, Birth, Growth
Beltane	1st May	Fertility, Luck, Pleasure, Sacred Marriage
Litha	21st June	Activity, Life, Strength
Lughnasadh	1st August	Harvest (Grain), Sacrifice, Transformation
Modron	21st September	Abundance, Balance, Harvest (Fruit)

Purifying & Consecrating Tools

Whenever you buy or make a new ritual tool, or indeed purchase one second-hand, you need to purify (cleanse) and consecrate (empower) it. Cleansing removes any influences from the tool so it is psychically clean when you start to work with it. Consecration focuses the energies of the elements into a tool, and establishes it as a magickal item that will only be used for your magickal work.

Elemental Purification & Consecration

The following is a ritual which can be used to purify and consecrate all your tools as well as items such as candles. Remember you can adapt the ritual to suit your circumstances – it can also be done as part of a Sabbat celebration or an Esbat.

Set up your altar in your usual manner, including salt & water in bowls, one red candle and some incense or joss sticks. Purify your ritual space, cast a circle, invoke the Elemental Guardians and invoke the Goddess and the God.

Pass the item through the incense smoke (if it is large you may move the censer around it and blow smoke over it as well as you do this), saying:

> *I purify you with the power of the element of Air.*

As you do this visualise winds blowing over the item, removing any impurities.

Pass the item through a candle flame, saying:

> *I purify you with the power of the element of Fire.*

As you do this visualise fire caressing the item around its edges, burning away any impurities.

Sprinkle the item with water, saying:

I purify you with the power of the element of Water.

As you do this visualise water flowing over and around the item, washing away any impurities.

Sprinkle the item with salt saying:

I purify you with the power of the element of Earth.

As you do this visualise the item being surrounded with earth, absorbing any impurities.

After you have purified your tool, you will need to empower it and consecrate it for the purpose you intend to use it for. Pass the item through each of the elemental representations on your altar as before:

Pass the item through the incense, saying:

I consecrate and charge you with the powers of the element of Air.

As you do this, visualise the wind filling the tool with the wisdom of Air.

Pass the item through the candle flame, saying:

I consecrate and charge you with the powers of the element of Fire.

As you do this, visualise the Fire tempering it with the creative power of Fire.

Sprinkle the item with water, saying:

I consecrate and charge you with the powers of the element of Water.

As you do this, visualise Water filling it with the tides of emotional balance.

Sprinkle the item with salt, saying:

> *I consecrate and charge you with the powers of the element of Earth.*

As you do this, visualise the endurance and stability of Earth entering the item.

Finally hold the item up towards the symbolic representations of the Goddess and God on your altar and saying:

> *I consecrate and charge you with the powers divine*
> *May the might of the God always be thine*
> *May the wisdom of the Goddess your purpose define*
> *To serve my intent my will to refine.*
>
> *So mote it be!*

After you have purified and consecrated your tool, you should wrap it in silk, or if you prefer any other natural fabric, such as wool, cotton or linen, to help preserve the charge. It is also an old belief that your tools should never be touched by another person,   the only exception being if it is a tool which is being shared in a group ritual.

Posture

When you meet a person for the first time, one of the subtle cues you pick up off them is how they hold themselves. Do they stand proud and upright, or slouch and look like they want to hide in a corner? How you react to a person will be influenced by their posture and body language.

Likewise how you hold yourself when performing magick is very important. You should never slouch! When you are standing up, hold your back straight and upright. This helps the flow of energy in your body, which you obviously want to optimise when performing magick.

In the same way, when you are sitting to meditate, make sure that your back is straight and upright. Sloppy posture shows a lack of focus and may frustrate the energy you are trying to focus to make your magick work.

Putting a cushion under your buttocks when you sit cross-legged makes it easier to sit comfortably for longer, and means that you will be less likely to become distracted by aches or pins and needles. Likewise if you practice sitting against a wall, you will soon get used to the posture you assume when you have your back straight.

When you are sitting meditating, rest your hands gently on your knees, palms upwards. This shows that your energy is flowing outwards into your magick circle. If however the meditation is purely internal, you may wish to place your hands palms down, to make your body a closed energy circuit, keeping all the energy circulating just within you.

Where appropriate you can form your hands into hand postures appropriate to the energy of your work. A common hand posture to use is to have the thumbs resting on the nail of the (bent) forefingers, with the other three fingers of each hand slightly curled. This represents the control of the ego (symbolised by the forefinger) by the higher self (symbolised by the thumb).

Do not lie down to meditate, as this may result in you falling asleep! You should sit cross-legged, if you can manage it comfortably. If sitting on the ground is going to be a problem, have a chair in the circle that you can sit in to meditate or for quiet parts of the ritual.

It should be a chair rather than a stool, so your back can be straight and upright against the back of the chair. Traditionally when sitting in a chair the hands are placed palms down on the thighs, with the fingertips just reaching the knees. This position helps you maintain your focus and promotes good energy flow.

Magickal Gestures

Earlier we have already mentioned elemental pentagrams, which are a form of magickal gesture. There are many other magickal gestures, some which can be seamlessly incorporated into Wiccan ritual with great effect. Movement implies action and change, and when you do Wicca this is what you are making happen. Hence it is a good idea to look at the gestures you make, as you can use them to symbolise particular energies and actions, helping your mind focus more clearly on the intent of what you are doing.

You can use existing hand gestures, or create your own to add focus to your rituals. Each of the fingers has an attribution, as do the phalanges of each finger. Moving from the fingertip towards the palm, the phalanges correspond to spirit, mind and body. Hence you can see that rings are generally worn on the physical (body) part of the finger.

Finger	Affects	Planet
Thumb	Will, Intent	-
Forefinger	Action, Direction, Path	Jupiter
Middle or Big Finger	Inspiration, Intuition	Saturn
Ring Finger	Creativity	Sun
Little Finger	Change, Opportunity	Mercury

The other three classical planets are represented by areas on the palm of the hand. The Mount of Venus is the fleshy area around the thumb, the central area of the hand corresponds to Mars, and the mound on the lower outer edge of the palm is the Mount of the Moon.

By touching the thumb, representing will, to the appropriate area of the palm, or to the appropriate finger, you can focus your intent with an appropriate planetary hand gesture. Hence touching the thumb to the little finger would indicate a Mercurial focus, to the middle finger a Saturnian focus, to the centre of the palm a Martial focus, etc.

It is easier to keep the other fingers straight, and bend the planetary finger to meet the thumb, when making gestures for the planets corresponding to the fingers, and likewise keep them straight when touching the thumb to the areas of the palm.

These gestures can just be used for devotional and meditation work if you find they distract rather than focus your mind when performing magickal work. As with other things in magick, it is about finding what works for you, so that you can develop a fluid and efficient style for performing your rituals, where your actions and the symbolism behind them all make sense to you.

The Elemental Gestures

Although this is not traditionally a part of Wicca, we are including the Elemental gestures we use in our training circle here, as they are excellent ways for a group to focus their minds on the elemental energies when the quarters are being called.

When performing group ritual, the rest of the group can make these gestures, whilst the person invoking the elemental guardian will still perform the gestures with their arms described previously. When working by yourself, you can decide which way suits you best by experimenting with both.

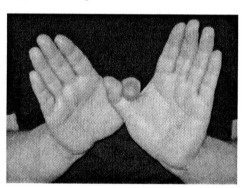

Air

Interlocked thumbs, making a bird like gesture to symbolise the element of Air.

Fire

Thumbs together with forefingers forming the apex of an upright triangle, which is the symbol of the element of Fire.

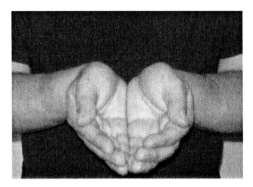

Water

Hands cupped together, as if scooping water, to symbolise the element of Water.

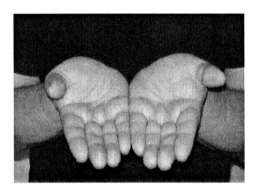

Earth

Hands side-by-side, completely flat, to symbolise the stability of the element of Earth.

Another set of elemental gestures you can perform are to make the elemental signs using your hands. For these you make the triangle shapes that correspond to each element. You may find you prefer these as they provide a sense of more obvious uniformity and connection between the four gestures.

These four elemental signs are taken from the hexagram[2], and show how it represents the universe. For the combination of the four elements makes up everything in the physical universe, and this is reflected in these signs being formed from the hexagram.

---

[2] See Part V, "Some Magickal Symbols" for an explanation

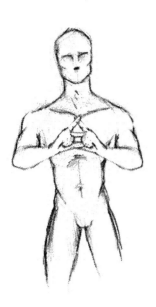

Air

Make an upward pointing triangle, with your thumbs touching at the tips forming the base of the triangle and your fingers steepling up to make the two other sides of the triangle. The big fingers should be lowered so one rests on the other horizontally, parallel to the thumbs. Note that the little fingers do not actually have to touch finger tips, they should just be next to the ring fingers.

Fire

Again make an upward pointing triangle, with your thumbs touching at the tips forming the base, and the fingers steepling up to make the two other sides of the triangle.

Water

Turn your hands so they face downwards, and put your thumbs touching at the tips so they form the horizontal base of the triangle. The fingers steeple downwards forming the two downward pointing sides of the triangle.

Earth

Turn your hands so they face downwards, and put your thumbs touching at the tips so they form the horizontal base of the triangle. Steeple the fingers as for the water gesture, but move the big fingers to the horizontal so one rests on the other making a horizontal bar parallel to the horizontal upper side of the triangle.

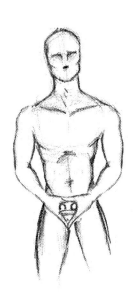

Elemental Pentagrams

The Elements are attributed to the points of the pentagram, clockwise, starting with Spirit at the top, Water, Fire, Earth and Air. The elemental pentagrams are used by the person invoking the Elemental Guardians and are drawn as gateways through which the elemental energies can enter the circle.

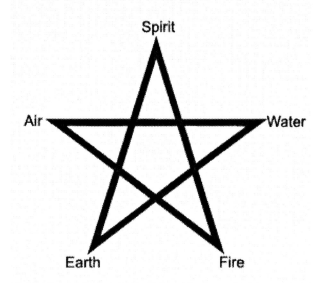

When you draw a pentagram, it should be a reasonable size. Hold your arm out straight, and imagine the five points in the air in front of you corresponding to the equivalent positions in front of your head, left and right shoulders, and left and right hips. That is where the point of your tool or your fingers should be in the air, making a pentagram that is several foot across.

E.g., if you were performing the invoking Earth pentagram, you start with your arm held out so your preferred hand is in front of the top of your head. You then bring the arm down diagonally left so the hand is in front of your left hip, then diagonally up right so the hand is in front of your right shoulder. Continue the stroke horizontally to the left so your hand is in front of your left shoulder, and then bring it down

Invoking Elemental Pentagrams

Air   Fire

Water   Earth

Banishing Elemental Pentagrams

Air   Fire

Water   Earth

diagonally right to be in front of your right hip. Finish the pentagram by bringing your hand up diagonally left so it returns to its starting place in front of your crown.

You should keep your arm straight at all times, and the movements should be fluid rather than jerky, so it is a single continuous flowing stroke. If you find this difficult, practice until it is second nature.

The purpose of the use of the elemental pentagrams when invoking the guardians of the watchtowers is to help bring those guardians into the circle. The pentagrams themselves act as both a doorway for the Guardians to enter through, as well as additional protection for the circle itself.

The use of the elemental pentagrams is a personal choice, some groups choose to use them, others, use only the invoking and banishing Earth pentagrams, some omit them altogether.

Elemental pentagrams serve as doorways for the force of the element to enter through or depart. In addition to their use in the calling of the Watchtowers, they are also sometimes used in blessing rituals and spells (to represent that particular elemental energy).

If you prefer you can visualise the pentagrams in the corresponding colour of the element instead of them all being gold. So for instance, you can visualise a golden yellow pentagram for Air, a fiery red pentagram for Fire, a shiny blue pentagram for Water and a forest green pentagram for Earth.

The Elemental Landscapes

When you draw elemental pentagrams, you are opening a doorway into your circle for the forces of that element. To help with this process, you can visualise the elemental landscape for that element through the pentagon in the middle of the pentagram.

As you do this you will feel the energy of that element entering your circle. For Air this may manifest as a breeze rushing past you, for Fire a sudden sense of heat, for Water a sense of moistness in the air around you, and for Earth a feeling of solidity and heaviness.

Air Landscape
The Air landscape is actually more of a skyscape. See a blue sky, with white clouds in it. Different types of birds fly through the sky, and you may also see mythical flying creatures like pegasi or griffins.

Fire Landscape
The Fire landscape is a hot sandy desert. Running through the desert you see a river of molten lava from a volcano in the distance. There are also trees with red bark, whose leaves are all individual flames. Creatures such as lizards, snakes and salamanders may be seen, as well as mythical creatures like the phoenix and basilisk.

Water Landscape
The Water landscape is a coastline. A river runs over a cliff, forming a waterfall down into the sea below, which ebbs and flows with its tides. In the water you may see creatures like dolphins and whales, fish and seals, as well as mythical creatures like mermaids and sea goats.

Earth Landscape
The Earth landscape is a mountain range, with a forest on the lower levels of the mountains. All different sorts of trees may be seen in the forest, which is filled with creatures like deer and boar, bears and lynx. You may also see mythical creatures like gnomes, nymphs, fauns and dryads.

Using your Voice

Your voice is one of the most powerful magickal tools you possess, and you always have it handy. The power of sound has been well documented by science, and from a magickal perspective sound can be considered to be transmutable energy. How you speak or sing words can dramatically affect the quality of your ritual.

Words contain an inherent power. With words we communicate, and by naming something you begin to gain an understanding of that thing. Magickal names have been considered important since the idea of true names giving power over beings in ancient Egypt.

Considering the importance of words, you can see that the more energy you put into your words, the more you can add to your rituals. When you speak it should be clearly, so that each word is pronounced in a distinct way. Remember that the influence of your magick (and hence your words) will echo through the subtle planes. As a result you want those words to have a strong and positive charge on them.

Practice projecting your voice, so it fills the room when you are indoors. This is not just a matter of shouting or being very loud – you do not have to be that loud to fill a space, and on many occasions this can be inappropriate.

As well as speaking clearly, you also need to consider the use of songs and chants. Since ancient times the value of repetition in magick has been recognised. As chants are one of the ways of raising energy, you need to spend some time performing them to really get a good level of energy up to power spells.

In some religious ceremonies, such as those of Hinduism or Buddhism, sacred mantras (a word or phrase) are chanted for hours. Whilst we are not saying you should spend hours performing your chants, you can appreciate that singing a chant for two minutes is going to raise a lot less energy than doing it for ten minutes.

When you do use your voice, it is important that you also keep in mind the intent of your ritual. Practising ritual teaches you (if you didn't already have the skill) to be able to split your attention and multi-task. Through practice it becomes easy to hold an image in your mind and use your voice, perform ritual actions, etc.

Do not be afraid to really use your voice. If it makes you feel self-conscious, this is something you need to deal with and overcome. Through words our ideas can be given form, and manifested into the desired result of our intent, so speak the words of creation and let your goals become real.

PART V - Appendixes

Important Symbols

Pentagram

The Pentagram is the best known symbol used in modern Wicca. It represents balance and the perfection of the self. The five points represent the five elements – Air, Fire, Water, Earth with Spirit at the top. They also represent the five senses of man, the five limbs – legs, arms and head. It can also be seen as representing the five fingers on a hand or the five toes on a foot. It is used in consecrations and blessings, as well as in invocations. It is also used as a protection and doorway for the elemental guardians.

Hexagram

The hexagram, or six-pointed star, represents the Universe. It also encapsulates the axiom "As Above, So Below" which is represented by its two interlocking triangles, one pointing up and one pointing down. The downward pointing triangle represents the Goddess and the element of Water, the upward pointing triangle represents the God and the element of Fire. The upward pointing triangle, combined with the horizontal baseline of the other triangle, represents the element of Air. The downward pointing triangle with the horizontal line of the upwards pointing triangle represents the element of Earth. Thus the hexagram combines the symbols of all four of the elements, which comprise the totality of the material universe.

| Air | Fire | Water | Earth |

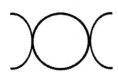

The Goddess

This symbol is sometimes used to represent the Goddess as the three-fold Maiden, Mother & Crone, but we use it as a general symbol to represent the ever changing nature of the Goddess, who like the Moon may take on many different roles at different times during the myths and during our lives. The Goddess can also be represented by just a simple crescent moon symbol.

The Horned God

This symbol is used to represent the Horned God, it is also of course the astrological symbol for the sunsign of Taurus. The Crescent can be seen as representing the horns of the God, whereas the circle can be seen as representing the Sun which is often associated with the Horned God in the Wiccan Tradition.

Ankh

The Egyptian symbol for life, which is often worn by Wiccans as a symbol of their devotion to the Gods, especially if they work with the Goddesses and Gods of the Egyptian pantheon. The Ankh is believed to have provided the inspiration for the Venus symbol as used in astrology. Venus is of course also a feminine planet, and as such the Ankh could be used to symbolise the feminine divine.

Colour Correspondences

Red	Red symbolises courage, danger, dynamism, energy, motivation, passion, self esteem, sexual love, stimulation, success, willpower and vitality. Red has been used to write down names of beings like Gods and angels since the time of ancient Egypt, to signify their power. Red cords or threads are associated with spirits and ethereal beings. Red is associated with the planet Mars and the element of Fire.
Orange	Orange symbolises communication, creativity, courage, dealing with trauma, developing self-esteem, emotional strength, improving luck, inspiration, knowledge, legal matters, prosperity, stimulating fertility and travel. Orange is associated with the planet Mercury.
Yellow	Yellow symbolises communication, emotional balance, enlightenment, harmony, improving memory, mental stimulation, travel and wealth. Yellow is the most reflective of colours and helps introspection. Yellow is associated with the Sun and the element of Air.
Green	Green symbolises balance, beauty, envy, fertility, growth, harmony, nature, nurture, serenity, truth. Green is the colour of plant life as the colour of the pigment chlorophyll used for photosynthesis. Green is associated with the planet Venus and the element of Earth.
Blue	Blue symbolises clarity, cleansing, enlightenment, healing, improving perception, meditation, mental calm, protection, purification, sincerity, success, tranquillity, understanding, wisdom. Blue is the first colour we register when seeing colours, and hints at the spiritual, hence its use in healing and circle casting visualisation. Blue is associated with the planet Jupiter and the element of Water.

Indigo	Indigo symbolises overcoming negative emotions, new perspectives and wisdom. Indigo is associated with the planet Jupiter. It may also be used to represent the element of Spirit.
Violet/ Purple	Violet and purple symbolise ambition, astral work, compassion, countering depression, developing psychic abilities, holistic balance of mind, body and spirit, illumination, improving luck, nobility, power, realisation, spiritual development, spiritual love. It is associated with the planet Uranus and the element of Spirit. It may also be used to represent the Moon.
Pink	Pink symbolises balance, beauty, calming, fidelity, friendship, gentleness, harmony, honour, integration, love, romance, subtlety and tranquillity. Pink is a colour of opposites – it can feel both cool ("cool pink") or hot ("shocking pink"). It is associated with the planet Venus, and may also be associated with the Sun (Qabalistic attribution).
Turquoise	Turquoise symbolises calm, good luck, joy, perfection, purity, serenity and spiritual harmony. Turquoise is associated with the planet Jupiter, and can represent the element of Air as the Sky.
Brown	Brown symbolises decisiveness, endurance, grounding, patience, practicality, security, stability, tolerance. Brown is associated with the element of Earth and is sometimes used to represent the planet Saturn.
White	White symbolises blessing, calming stress and negative emotion, change, chastity, cleanliness, completion, healing, innocence, perfection, purity, sacredness, spirit, spirituality, truth and wisdom. White is the reflection of all colours, and when split contains the entire spectrum of colours of the rainbow, so it is ideal for transformation of the self. White is often associated with divinity and as such can represent the element of Spirit. White is also associated with the planet Pluto, and is sometimes used as a Lunar colour. Also the element of Water as Ice.

Black	Black symbolises absorbing negativity, assertiveness, binding, bringing things to an end, dealing with depression and grief, divination, focus, protection, unmanifest potential. As the absorption of all colours, black is a very protective colour (or more correctly absence of colour). Black is associated with the planet Saturn and the element of Spirit. Confusingly it is also sometimes attributed to the element of Earth.
Grey	Grey symbolises neutrality and dispelling negative influences. Grey is associated with the planet Neptune, and is also sometimes used to symbolise the Moon. Grey and silver are sometimes used interchangeably.
Silver	Silver symbolises astral and dream work, developing psychism, skrying and versatility. Silver is associated with the Moon. Silver and white are sometimes used interchangeably.
Gold	Gold symbolises achieving goals, healing, prosperity, success and wealth. Gold is associated with the Sun. Gold and yellow are sometimes used interchangeably.

Numerical Correspondences

One	Number of unity, of totality. One is often considered the number of the divine spirit, as the all-pervading energy of life, beyond gender or any division. It is the beginning, the initial manifestation from nothingness. It can only be divided by itself, and is a factor of every other whole number, showing the divine spirit in everything. One is also the number of the self, of the individual, as when you talk about yourself in the first person. It can be seen as a number of self-sufficiency, of the single individual. It represents the point as the first depiction of existence.
Two	Number of duality, of the polarity of opposites. Polarities are dualistic, so we have Goddess-God, light-dark, female-male, day-night, black-white, positive-negative, action-reaction, etc. A complimentary number, for balance is achieved by the union of opposite polarities, and this can be seen mostly clearly in relationships. In Wicca two is often considered a masculine number, as the horns of the Horned God. Two is a number of choice, for there is no longer a single perspective, you have to choose, and may be on the "horns of a dilemma". Represents the line, which can be seen as the lingam or phallus, the masculine energy.
Three	Trinity, where the union of opposites produces a third, complementary force. In Wicca three is often considered a feminine number, as the triple aspect of Maiden, Mother and Crone. It can also be seen as the number of the Child of Promise, the result of the union of Goddess and God. The number of Saturn, and form, as it gives us the first shape, the triangle. A very common magickal number as the three principles of life, death and rebirth, or earth, sky and underworld, the three Fates, the three Graces, etc.
Four	Four is the quaternary, the square or equal armed cross. The number of stability, as the solidity of the square. Balance and hence the four elements and the four directions. With four we move into three dimensions with the tetrahedron, and the fourth dimension of time is implied, as once something has form, it exists within the dimensions of space, and has duration. Also two squared, again indicating stability. The number of Jupiter.

Five	Number of man, the microcosm. Five represents the manifestation of spirit in matter, the pentagram, and hence can be seen as a number of activity and movement. Five is also the elements all together in harmony – Air, Fire, Water, Earth and Spirit. Can also be seen as the number of the sacred marriage, of the masculine two with the feminine three, hence the five points of fellowship when two people embrace. We have five physical senses, and five digits on each of our extremities, so five is very much the generic number for humanity. The number of Mars.
Six	Six is the number of the universe, the macrocosm. The hexagram, which is two times three, and as such represents the balance of the Goddess and God as the downward and upward pointing triangles. Six is a number of perfection, being the only number produced by both adding and multiplying its factors (1+2+3, 1x2x3). The number of the Sun. The cube also symbolises six, with its six faces.
Seven	Number of completion, and has always been considered one of the most mystical of numbers. Seven days in a week, seven colours in a rainbow, seven notes in a musical scale, seven major chakras, seven classical planets, the list goes on and on. The number of Venus and is thus associated with love. It is also considered a mystical number, uniting the divine triplicity with the material and solid four.
Eight	Considered to be a magickal number, representing as it does the Mercurial energy of change, communication and healing. Also a number of solidity, being the first cube number (2 x 2 x 2), and if you look at a cube you will see it has eight corners. For these reasons eight is also a number of fullness.
Nine	Lunar number, connected with cycles and completion, being the last simple number before 10, and also because nine is unique in that any number multiplied by nine will always generate a product that adds up to nine. There are nine planets in our solar system, and nine is attributed to groups of beings, such as nine Muses, nine Orders of Angels, etc. It is 3 x 3, and is hence seen as a Goddess number. This is also reinforced by the nine month gestation of pregnancy in women.

Ten	Number of balance and stability. It is the sum of the first four numbers, one, two, three and four. As such it represents all the elements in balance, and this is why it is the number of the planet Earth. Ten is the number base we work in, based on our ten fingers, and there are ten spheres on the Tree of Life. Ten indicates an increase in scale, beyond simple numbers. Ten is also the original unity extended into full manifestation (indicated by the circle of the 0 after the 1), embodying the principle of "As above, so below".
Eleven	Eleven is considered to be the number of magick. It is the one beyond ten, the invisible influence of subtle energies. The first number formed by repetition – 1 and 1, symbolising the creative tension between two opposing forces, the polarity which underlies magick. It is also the first number which adds together to form something different (two), implying change. Eleven is also the number of Uranus.
Twelve	Twelve is the number of the zodiac, and is hence a stellar number. We have twelve months in the solar year (and of course our Sun is a star). A number of completion, the whole cycle, and is the result of the feminine three multiplied by the masculine four.
Thirteen	A lunar number, due to the thirteen Moons in a year. Thirteen is also the sum of four and nine, the squares of two and three, making it a number of union.
Twenty-Two	Twenty-two is considered a magickal number due to its Qabalistic connection. There are twenty-two paths on the Tree of Life, Hebrew letters and Tarot trumps. It is also the product of two and eleven, implying change of an even greater magnitude than eleven.

Planetary Correspondences

The Sun

Colours	Gold, orange, yellow
Direction	South
Tools	Sword
Scents	Chamomile, cinnamon, frankincense, ginger, juniper, rosemary
Crystals	Amber, diamond, orange calcite, sunstone, topaz, zircon
Metal	Gold
Numbers	6, 36
Rules	Leo
Intent	Advancement, charisma, friendship, growth, harmony, healing, individuality, leadership, power, success, wealth, will.

The Moon

Colours	Silver, white
Direction	North-West
Tools	Magick Mirror
Scents	Aniseed, camphor, jasmine, myrrh, ylang ylang
Crystals	Chalcedony, moonstone, pearl, quartz
Metal	Silver
Numbers	9, 13, 28, 81
Rules	Cancer
Intent	Astral work, birth, cycles, dreams, fertility, intuition, mystery, psychic ability, reconciliation, secrets, spells, tides.

The Earth

Colours	Black, brown, green
Direction	North-East
Tools	Drum
Scents	Patchouli, pine, vetivert
Crystals	Amber, aventurine, chrysocolla, emerald, jadeite, nephrite, onyx, staurolite
Metal	N/A – Horn is often used
Number	10, 100
Rules	-
Intent	Awareness, endurance, form, home, manifestation, nature, patience, perseverance, solidity, strength, tolerance.

Mercury

Colours	Orange, yellow, multi colours
Direction	East
Tools	Caduceus
Scents	Caraway, eucalyptus, lavender, lemon, lime, sandalwood
Crystals	Agate, citrine quartz, opal
Metal	Mercury
Number	8, 64
Rules	Gemini, Virgo
Intent	Business, commerce, communication, creativity, divination, exams, healing, humour, intelligence, knowledge, literature, memory, recovering lost property, science, travel.

Venus

Colours	Green, pink
Direction	Centre
Tools	Girdle
Scents	Benzoin, geranium, lotus, pennyroyal, peppermint, rose
Crystals	Emerald, jadeite, malachite, nephrite, peridot, rose quartz, zoisite
Metal	Copper
Number	7, 49
Rules	Libra, Taurus
Intent	Art, attraction, beauty, culture, emotions, enhancing friendship, fertility, harmony, love, peace, pleasure, sexuality.

Mars

Colours	Red
Direction	South-West
Tools	Spear
Scents	Basil, black pepper, ginger, hyssop, rue
Crystals	Garnet, hematite, heliotrope, magnetite, ruby, spinel
Metal	Iron
Number	5, 25
Rules	Aries, co-rules Scorpio
Intent	Conflict, courage, discord, drive, ego, military matters, passion, revenge, strength, vigour.

Jupiter

Colours	Blue, purple
Direction	South-East
Tools	Sceptre, wand
Scents	Cedar, hyssop, sandalwood
Crystals	Lapis lazuli, sapphire, sodalite, turquoise
Metal	Tin
Number	4, 16
Rules	Sagittarius, co-rules Pisces
Intent	Ambition, authority, business, career, devotion, good health, honour, humour, law, leadership, luck, obtaining friendship, philosophy, politics, religion, success, truth.

Saturn

Colours	Black, brown
Direction	North
Tools	Sickle, scythe
Scents	Camphor, lavender, myrrh
Crystals	Coral, jet, obsidian, onyx, smoky quartz
Metal	Lead
Number	3
Rules	Capricorn, co-rules Aquarius
Intent	Death, form, formation, history, limitation, memory, self-discipline, time, wisdom.

Uranus

Colours	Purple
Direction	Above
Tools	-
Scents	Cinnamon, clove, garlic
Crystals	Amethyst, kunzite, labradorite, opal, tourmaline
Metal	Tungsten
Number	11, 121
Rules	Co-rules Aquarius
Intent	Change, higher self, invention, magick, revolution, transformation.

Neptune

Colours	Grey, sea green
Direction	West
Tools	Trident
Scents	Ambergris, lemon
Crystals	Aquamarine, beryl, coral, pearl, prase
Metal	Titanium
Number	2
Rules	Co-rules Pisces
Intent	Compassion, mysticism, psychic powers, tides.

Pluto

Colours	Black, white
Direction	Below
Tools	-
Scents	Patchouli
Crystals	Diamond, jadeite, kunzite, zircon
Metal	Platinum
Number	1
Rules	Co-rules Scorpio
Intent	Death, regeneration, transmutation, unconscious, underworld.

Avalonia's Homestudy Course

If you are interested in learning more about Wicca and furthering your own understanding and experience of the tradition, you may be interested in the homestudy course written by Sorita D'Este and David Rankine for Avalonia.

It is a structured course which can be studied from anywhere in the world – by post or by email.   You will learn a wide range of techniques and will be guided throughout by a personal mentor who you can contact if you need help or advice with the course material or further explanation.

The course is based on the training programme used by the authors for members of their own covens prior to first degree initiation into their covens.

For more information please visit:
www.avalonia.co.uk

Or write to:
Avalonia Homestudy Course
BM Avalonia
London
WC1N 3XX
England

OTHER BOOKS BY THESE AUTHORS

The Guises of The Morrígan
The Irish Goddess of Sex & Battle – Her Myths, Powers & Mysteries
David Rankine & Sorita D'Este
Avalonia, 2005 – ISBN 1-905297-00-9

WICCA – Magickal Beginnings
The Evolution of a modern Witchcraft tradition
Sorita D'Este & David Rankine
Avalonia, 2005 – ISBN 1-90529703-03

ARTEMIS
Virgin Goddess of the Sun & Moon
Sorita D'Este
Avalonia, 2005 – ISBN 1-905297-02-5

Climbing The Tree of Life
A Handbook of Practical Magickal Qabalah
David Rankine
Avalonia, 2005 – ISBN 1-905297-02-7

Becoming Magick
New & Revised Magicks for the New Aeon
David Rankine
Mandrake of Oxford, 2004 – ISBN 1-869928-81-4

The Practical Angel Magic of Dr. John Dee's Enochian Tables
Tabula Bonorum Angelorum Invocationes
Stephen Skinner & David Rankine
Golden Hoard Press, 2004 – ISBN 0-954763-90-4

Crystals – Healing & Folklore
The uses and symbolism of crystals in folklore, myths and religion
David Rankine
Capall Bann Publishing, 2002 - ISBN 1-861632-00-2

Circle of Fire

Printed in the United Kingdom
by Lightning Source UK Ltd.
119336UK00001BA/1

9 781905 297047